DWIGHT K. NELSON

PURSUING THE PASSION OF JESUS

How "loving the least" helps you fulfill God's purpose for your life

Pacific Press® Publishing Association
Nampa, Idaho
Oshawa, Ontario, Canada
www.pacificpress.com

Designed by Michelle C. Petz
Front cover photo (bottom right): © Brian A. Vikander / CORBIS

Copyright © 2005 by
Pacific Press® Publishing Association
Printed in United States of America
All rights reserved

Additional copies of this book are available by calling toll free
1-800-765-6955 or visiting http://www.adventistbookcenter.com

Unless otherwise indicated,
all scriptural references are from the *New International Version*.

Library of Congress Cataloging-in-Publication Data

Nelson, Dwight K. Nelson.
p. cm.
Includes bibliographical references.
ISBN 0-8163-2043-8
1. Compassion—Religious aspects—Christianity. 2. Love—Religious aspects—
Christianity. 3. Christian life. 4. Bible. O.T. Issiah LVIII—Criticism, interpreta-
tion, etc. I. Title.

BV4647.S9N45 2005
242'.5—dc22   2004057327

05 06 07 08 09 · 5 4 3 2 1

DEDICATION

To the students of Andrews University
Whose passion for Jesus
And love for the poor
Have taught me

CONTENTS

Acknowledgments

This book has been a collaborative project from the beginning. Eight years ago, students here at Andrews University began to take seriously the needs of a nearby inner city, and their incarnational ministry on its streets and in its neighborhoods has affected not only their campus, but also their pastor. My dedication page expresses my gratitude to them.

But I'm also grateful to Ralph Watts, Jr., who while he was president of the international humanitarian ministry, Adventist Development and Relief Agency (ADRA), kept challenging me to grapple with the biblical call to serve the poor—locally, nationally, and globally. His idea for this book came over dinner one day. And I'm grateful for the partnership with him this project has facilitated. That he is my mother's kid brother, of course, has made the collaboration all the more delightful. Thank you, Uncle Ralph and Aunt Pat.

Russell Holt and his team of editors at Pacific Press Publishing Association have once again made writing for them a joy. Thank you, Russ, for helping vision this project into reality, and for providing the study guides at the end of the book—the combination of which will make for some spirited small group discussions, I am certain!

All my preaching and writing are a collaboration with a congregation I've been blessed and privileged to pastor since 1983. There are no people on earth like those at the Pioneer Memorial Church. Through the years we've wrestled together with the radical call of God. This book is a measure of how we have covenanted together to follow Him. Thank you for the journey.

And finally, my wife Karen's partnership in ministry has turned theory into practice, as together we've spent Sabbath afternoons walking the streets of an inner-city block we've adopted as our own. She knows the names and the needs of those who live on this street. And they know her love, as do I. And for that I'll be grateful forever.

FOREWORD

The world in which we live today is littered with the wreckage of human suffering. Anywhere we look, we find disease, destruction, death, and despair. Such a picture of world conditions is certainly not appealing, but it is realistic. The HIV/AIDS epidemic, as well as the ravages caused by measles and other diseases, is creating personal tragedy and widespread havoc in many areas of the world. One result is that thousands of orphans are being left for society to care for. Add to this the destruction caused by such natural disasters as earthquakes, typhoons, hurricanes, and the terrible cyclones that devastate Bangladesh and other areas of southeast Asia, leaving tens of thousands of families homeless. Man-made strife increases the suffering further—the genocide of Rwanda and the Sudan, not to mention the conflicts in Afghanistan and Iraq together with all the death, destruction, and despair associated with them.

As Christians, how should we respond? What obligation—individually and corporately—do we have to the poor, the sick, the displaced, the disadvantaged, the downtrodden? I believe this book, with its call to action in this area, will help stimulate your thinking about these issues and point you to answers.

The conviction that such a book is needed has been growing in my heart over the years. As a church administrator, I served the church in

Korea following the Korean War and then in southeast Asia during the Indo-China conflict. In more recent years, I have been the president of the Adventist Development and Relief Agency (ADRA) and have visited nearly every area of major conflict upon this battered planet. At times I have had the opportunity of sharing my concerns for humanitarian needs with my nephew, Dwight Nelson, senior pastor of the Pioneer Memorial Church in Berrien Springs, Michigan. As we discussed these issues, I urged him to think of developing a series of messages in which he could articulate a viable Christian response to human need in light of what the Scriptures have to say about how Christians should respond to the plight of those who are suffering from emotional, physical, and spiritual stress. Particularly, we need to take into account the example of our Lord Jesus who demonstrated His compassion for those at the margins of society. In Matthew 9:35, 36 we read how Jesus went about the cities and villages, teaching in the synagogues, proclaiming the gospel of His kingdom, and healing every kind—*every kind*—of disease and sickness. "And seeing the multitudes, he felt compassion for them because they were distressed and downcast like sheep without a shepherd."

The Scriptures, Old and New Testaments, are replete with counsel as to what our response should be to the plight of the poor in our homes, our churches, our communities, and throughout the world.

Is the task staggering? Absolutely. Can we solve all these issues? No. But we can make a start. We can make a difference—each one of us. I like the words of G. K. Chesterton who wrote, "The Christian ideal has not been tried and found wanting. It has been found difficult and left untried."

Yes, it has been found difficult. But as members of the Christian community, shall we not resolve that we will *not* leave this challenge untried?

Ralph S. Watts, Jr.
President, Adventist Development and Relief Agency
1985-2002

"Done While You Wait"

Our family was driving down to Florida for spring break when I saw a highway sign that made me do a double take. If you've driven through the South, you know that there are all kinds of roadside signs advertising everything from "See Rock City" (that celebrated tourist trap outside Chattanooga) to "Crazy Sam's" or "Deadeye Dick's" fireworks stand (since firecrackers are still legal in that region). But I had never seen *this* sign before. And so as we flew by it, Karen grabbed a pen and jotted it down before we could forget it.

It was a sign advertising a tattoo parlor—tattoos being the rage that they are these days. In giant red letters the name of the outfit stretched across the billboard, "Tattoo Charlie's." Then below came the slogan: "Done while you wait."

Wait a minute! "Done while you wait"? How else are you supposed to get a tattoo? Drop your arm off and pick it up at the end of the day all tattooed and ready to go? "Done while you wait." Is there any alternative? Pretty clever advertising, wouldn't you say? It certainly got my attention, anyway.

But come to think of it, the greatest truths in the universe can be posted on a roadside sign with the same slogan, can't they? "Done while you wait"—the shining truth of God's original creation of this planet of earth children; He did the work while we waited. "Done while you wait"—the resplendent truth of God's saving love poured out in the sacrificial death of Jesus on the cross for those same earth children; He did the work while we waited. One by one, you can check them off, the greatest themes and truths of the universe, clustered under the divine pronouncement, "Done while you wait." He does the work . . . we do the waiting . . . on Him.

What a God—what an offer—what a forever Friend!

But may I be candid with you? There is one truth that *can't* be done while we wait. In fact, it *won't* get done *if* we wait. Which may explain why God is still waiting—waiting for us to quit waiting. And start working.

Before you leap to your feet in valiant defense of salvation by faith, let me hasten to begin singing! And if the voice my family long ago relegated to occasions of hydrotherapy (the morning shower) won't stop you, then perhaps the words I sing to you will. They are the hymn composition of Fred Pratt Green:

When the church of Jesus Shuts its outer door,
Lest the roar of traffic Drown the voice of prayer:
May our prayers, Lord, make us Ten times more aware
That the world we banish Is our Christian care.

If our hearts are lifted Where devotion soars
High above this hungry Suffering world of ours:
Lest our hymns should drug us To forget its needs,
Forge our Christian worship Into Christian deeds.

Lest the gifts we offer, Money, talents, time,
Serve to salve our conscience To our secret shame:
Lord, reprove, inspire us By the way You give;
Teach us, dying Savior, How true Christians live.[1]

"When the church of Jesus shuts its outer door." And waits. When in fact God is desperately hoping, passionately pleading, for us to quit waiting . . . and start working.

I love the church to which I belong. But I fear she waits when she should work. Drugged by her own hymns (*both* traditional and contemporary) and anesthetized by her weekly (weakly?) worship, does she sleep when she should serve? Is she contented when she should contend? Do we flee "the roar of traffic," when it's to that urban cacophony that we've been sent? Does the church (at least in the West) pray in opulent obscurity, when in fact we've been called to impoverished humanity? Are we forever seeking more signs, when the one sign left us is forgotten?

What about that sign writ large on an ancient piece of parchment, the sign of Isaiah 58? Everyone knows Isaiah, but who reads the fifty-eighth chapter any more? Jesus must have. For how else can you explain "the passion of the Christ" (Mel Gibson's movie notwithstanding)? The truth is you won't find God any more passionately engaged with His people in the Old Testament or Jesus any more passionate in appealing to the same people (that would be you and me) in the New Testament than they both are over Isaiah 58's red-hot appeal. Call it "the passion of the Father"; call it "the passion of the Son."

One thing's for certain. It is a passion whose time has come. Because God knows we appear to have mastered the waiting part. It's the working part that He's waiting for. "Done while you *work.*" Because there's no other way to get it done.

But if you think *w-o-r-k* spells bad news, guess again. If you will put into practice what you're about to read, research empirically shows that it will improve your health, boost your immune system, lengthen your life, grow your investments, strengthen your self-esteem, embolden your faith, deepen your prayers, increase your joy—in other words, it will literally revolutionize your personal life. Sound impossible? I hope you'll examine the evidence and studies cited for yourself in these pages. And if Isaiah 58's practical strategy has this kind of documented effect on us personally, can you imagine the corporate effect on the church?

But let me hasten to inject this caveat: This short book is not about some sort of new "health and wealth" scheme or gospel. Quite the contrary. Isaiah 58 is the cry of the divine heart not only for you and me. It is a cry ignited with the fire of His relentless love for all six billion plus of His earth children. And while you and I can do very little about the war on terror or the conflict in Iraq or the jittery national or global economy, what we can do is to take seriously God's compassion for His suffering children and His passionate longing that they, too, be included in an end-time portrait of His last generation on earth. Just what it is we *can* do and *might* do to share His passion for them is what this little book seeks.

It is a journey. We must begin. So let us embark together with the prayer of Fred Pratt Green: "Teach us, dying Savior, how true Christians live." After all, thanks to Mel Gibson's *The Passion of the Christ*, Jesus keeps dying a thousand times over on the screens of this nation and world. So it is the right time, isn't it, to ask this "dying Savior" "How, then, shall we live?"

In the few pages that follow, may Christ teach us how to do just that—to follow Him whose passion is why this book was written in the first place.

May Day, 2004
Dwight K. Nelson
Pioneer Memorial Church

---

[1] *Seventh-day Adventist Hymnal,* No. 581.

CHAPTER ONE

THE LAW OF
THE BOOKENDS

Did you hear what happened at the Seattle-Tacoma International Airport? It was the Sunday after New Year's Day, and the postholiday crowds were streaming through the terminal on their way home. According to the *South Bend Tribune* (January 6, 2003), one of the security screeners—the person who sits beside the X-ray machine and stares into the monitor to see how neatly you packed your carry-on luggage—apparently had been to one too many New Year's parties. In the middle of his security assignment in front of the X-ray monitor, he fell asleep. He may have done it with his eyes wide open—like it happens sometimes when you're driving down the interstate—but eventually someone noticed. Red alert!

The question now became: How long had he been asleep? He hadn't timed his nap, but through hurried questioning, his supervisor estimated he had been asleep from eight to thirty minutes. The authorities immediately shut down Sea-Tac airport. Four of the five concourses were evacuated, and thousands of passengers were delayed as explosive-sniffing dogs swept through the terminal to make certain no unknown terrorist had breached security during the agent's unintended siesta.

Moral of the story: It's a very serious matter to be found sleeping on the job when so many are depending on your being wide awake, when you have a strategic assignment. I can't imagine that sleepy security guard and his superior having a cheery little postnap chit-chat, can you?

Would it be any different with the ultimate Superior? Do you suppose that's why God sounds so deeply agitated in Isaiah 58's opening salvo? " 'Shout it aloud, do not hold back. Raise your voice like a trumpet. Declare to my people their rebellion and to the house of Jacob their sins' " (verse 1). After all, that doesn't exactly sound like a page from Dale Carnegie's *How to Win Friends and Influence People,* does it?

So much for our journey through Isaiah 58 getting off to a warm and fuzzy start.

But why such a harsh introduction? " 'Shout it aloud, do not hold back. Raise your voice like a trumpet. Declare to my people their rebellion and to the house of Jacob their sins.' "

Could it be that somebody's been sleeping on the job?

Richard John Neuhaus, editor-in-chief of *First Things: A Monthly Journal of Religion and Public Life,* writes in his provocative book *Death on a Friday Afternoon:* "God's chosen ones live out the drama and destiny of God himself. *It is a fearful thing to be chosen.* It is as though God enters history through his chosen ones" (p. 138, emphasis supplied).

Is that why Isaiah 58 begins with such divine agitation? As Neuhaus writes, "It is a fearful thing to be chosen." Because to whom much is given, much is required (see Luke 12:48). When you live with the thought that you've been chosen by God—not because of who *you* are, but because of who *He* is—you cannot content yourself to live like all the rest. You must live with a sense of destiny. You will live by a higher standard.

Wasn't it that way for Israel?

> For you are a people holy to the LORD your God. The LORD your God has chosen you out of all the peoples on the face of the earth to be his people, his treasured possession. The LORD did not set his affection on you and choose you because you were more numerous than other peoples, for you were the fewest of all peoples. But it was because the LORD loved you and kept the oath he swore to your forefathers that he brought you out with a mighty hand and redeemed you from the land of slavery, from the power of Pharaoh king of Egypt (Deuteronomy 7:6-8).

The Israelites were to live out their manifest destiny with the abiding sense that "the LORD your God has chosen you." It wasn't because of any prowess or might of their own; the Israelites were to live out their divine destiny with the compelling realization that they had been chosen and loved for the sake of mission—God's mission to save the entire race of lost earth children. God had to start with someone, so He began His mission by choosing Israel.

But as Neuhaus has observed, "It is a fearful thing to be chosen. It is as though God enters history through his chosen ones." Israel was to be the incarnation of divine love in and through a community of very human missionaries, as it were. God longed to enter into history through them. Then, at last, the rebel planet might know the truth about Him.

But apparently a whole generation of Israelites fell asleep on duty, dangerously compromising their strategic mission to the world. And when you fall asleep at so vital an assignment, you can forget any postnap warm fuzzies from your ultimate Superior.

I'll never forget that afternoon when, as a boy, I awakened from my nap and proceeded to disobey my missionary parents by putting on my brand-new maroon Sabbath shoes and sneaking out the door to play with my Japanese friends. I wanted to show off my shoes, and besides, what harm could a little week-day romping do? Soon all caution was thrown to the proverbial wind, as we boys raced through the muddy rice paddies near our home. Suddenly, my errant memory revived. I looked in horror at my now brown Sabbath shoes. In panic I raced back to the house, hoping to sneak in the back door and scrub them clean. But when I crawled through the hedge fence, who should be there in the yard, snapping some pictures, but my dad! And before I could duck away, he spotted me and waved me over to pose for the camera. *Maybe he won't even notice my shoes,* I secretly prayed. But of course, being a dad, he did. Since the camera was already set up on a tripod, he told me we'd have our picture taken together first, and *then* we'd talk. To this day I look at that old black-and-white photograph of my dad and me—his grin full and natural, mine tepid and forced—remembering the rather painful corporal "conversation" that took place as soon as that picture was snapped!

There are no warm postnap fuzzies with your ultimate Superior when you've blatantly disobeyed Him, no matter how loving He is. " 'Shout it aloud, do not hold back. Raise your voice like a trumpet. Declare to my people their rebellion and to the house of Jacob their sins' " (Isaiah 58:1). After all, these are the "my people" of God. And even a quick reading of Isaiah 58 reveals what that "my people" status actually means.

Number one, it means that you embrace God's Day of Atonement (judgment) "cleansing of the sanctuary" teaching. Key code words to that unique divine teaching are embedded into the opening salvo of Isaiah 58. The "trumpet" in "raise your voice like a trumpet" is *shophar* in the Hebrew. And only one liturgical feast day was heralded by the blasts of the *shophar*—Yom Kippur, or the Day of Atonement (see Leviticus 23:23-27).

And no sooner does God call for the "judgment" trumpet to be sounded than Israel quickly protests: " 'Why have we fasted,' they say [to God], 'and you have not seen it? Why have we humbled ourselves, and you have not noticed?' " (Isaiah 58:3). Their claim to fasting and humbling themselves is straight out of the ceremonial code book for acceptable Day of Atonement activities. "It [the Day of Atonement] is to be a sabbath of solemn rest for you, that you may *humble* your souls" (Leviticus 16:31, NASB, emphasis supplied). As God's "chosen ones" Israel unapologetically embraced the divine teaching of the Day of Atonement.

But that "my people" status with God also means that you embrace and revere the Creator's seventh-day Sabbath memorial. And Israel did that as well, as the ending to Isaiah 58 makes incontrovertibly clear:

> "If you keep your feet from breaking the Sabbath
> and from doing as you please on my holy day,
> if you call the Sabbath a delight
> and the LORD's holy day honorable,
> and if you honor it by not going your own way
> and not doing as you please or speaking idle words,

then you will find your joy in the LORD,
 and I will cause you to ride on the heights of the land
 and to feast on the inheritance of your father Jacob."
  The mouth of the LORD has spoken (Isaiah 58:13, 14).

There they are—the two bookends that frame Isaiah 58. Two unique divine teachings that comprise part of the spiritual DNA of God's chosen people. And Israel claimed them both!

Have you met anyone else—perhaps another spiritual community that you might know—that also claims them both?

"It is a fearful thing to be chosen." Why? Because to whom much is given, much is required. So "cry aloud" and "spare not," as the King James English renders it, and "shew my people their transgression." For they have forgotten what is required of the "chosen ones."

And what is required is much more than simply the bookends. For you see, neither God nor Isaiah here in chapter fifty-eight is attempting to prove either bookend. The veracity of the bookends (the cleansing of the sanctuary judgment and the seventh-day Sabbath memorial) isn't what's at stake in Isaiah 58.

What's at stake is what's *in between the bookends*. Have you ever gazed upon the hallowed shelves of a rare book collection? Isn't there a verse in the Bible somewhere that breathes the prayer, "May my days come to an end in the house of a book collector"? Perhaps not. But the sentiment surely belongs to every bibliophile. And as every lover of books knows, the great attraction in the shelved collections of rare books lies in the masterful artistry of the leather-bound and yellow-paged tomes held firmly and securely upright by the bookends. The beauty and glory of a shelf of rare books lie not in the bookends. What is of inestimable value is what is preserved *between* those bookends. That is the law of the bookends.

Isaiah 58 is not an ode to the bookends, as crucial as they are. Rather, it is God's passionate cry, calling us to turn our attention to what is *between His two bookends*.

And what is between them? The answer to that question is the rest of this book.

CHAPTER TWO

SMARTY-PANTS

I went to college with a kid who drove me crazy. He was always right. And it made me mad—because that's what *I* wanted to be. Always right. Is there anything more irritating than a smarty-pants? Let's face it. People who are always right can be a pain. I love Mark Twain's quip about them; he called them people "who are *good* in the *worst* sense of the word." Always right.

Is that what has happened to our church? Have we become what we abhor? Always right? Spiritual, ecclesiastical, theological smarty-pants?

To find the answer we need to watch God get steaming mad—without losing His temper, of course. The Scripture calls this His righteous "indignation" (see Psalm 78:49), His holy "wrath" (see Revelation 14:19). Here are three punchy, in-your-face stories with more than a few hints of an answer to our question—Have we become spiritual know-it-alls? This much is certain: I wouldn't want to have been there when these stories happened!

But before reliving these divine outbursts, hang on to two words that will provide the key for these three tales:

- **Orthodoxy.** [Greek: *orthos*—right, and *doxa*—opinion] thus, "right thinking" or "right believing."
- **Orthopraxy.** [Greek: *orthos*—right, and *praxis*—acts] thus, "right practicing" or "right behaving."

By definition, then, we could say that orthodoxy is *knowing* the truth and that orthopraxy is *showing* the truth. Makes you wonder, doesn't it, which one we do best—you and I? Knowing the truth or showing the truth? Orthodoxy or orthopraxy?

Now for those three explosive stories where God gets very angry. And I suppose you would, too, if you were He. All three stories feature "God with us"—that would be Jesus—and are told by Matthew. Let's read them from Eugene Peterson's *The Message* and check them out to see which way the orthodoxy-orthopraxy needle swings for us.

Story Number One

Jesus went straight to the Temple and threw out everyone who had set up shop, buying and selling. He kicked over the tables of loan sharks and the stalls of dove merchants. He quoted this text:

My house was designated a house of prayer;
You have made it a hangout for thieves.

Now there was room for the blind and crippled to get in. They came to Jesus and he healed them.

When the religious leaders saw the outrageous things he was doing, and heard all the children running and shouting through the Temple, "Hosanna to David's Son!" they were up in arms and took him to task. "Do you hear what these children are saying?"

Jesus said, "Yes, I hear them. And haven't you read in God's Word, 'From the mouths of children and babies I'll furnish a place of praise'?"

Fed up, Jesus turned on his heel and left the city for Bethany, where he spent the night (Matthew 21:12-17, *The Message*).

Jesus is not a very happy God in this story, is He? I don't know if He took up a rope whip there in that bizarre bazaar as He did when He cleansed the temple at the beginning of His ministry (see John

2:15). But Peterson's colorfully dramatic depiction of Jesus kicking over the loan sharks' tables hints of a pandemonium the temple hasn't witnessed since Herod rebuilt it! Bird feathers in the air and bird droppings on the ground. Sacrificial cattle in a panic and on the run (and you know what cows and sheep do when they're extremely nervous). Treasury tables upended and crashing onto the marble floor. The splatter and tinkle of temple shekels scattering in every direction. Temple bazaar merchants crazily tripping over each other and slipping in the cattle residue in their haste to flee the precincts. And one lone Man— His eyes ablaze, His voice thundering above the cacophony of the stampeding confusion: " 'It is written . . . "My house will be called a house of prayer," but you have made it a "den of robbers" ' " (Matthew 21:13).

Do you remember a television commercial years ago that quipped, "It's not wise to fool Mother Nature"? Well, the cleansing of the temple sanctuary certainly drove home the point, "It's not wise to anger Father God." No temper tantrum here, to be sure. Instead, the hot tears of a spurned Lover glisten in the catch in Jesus' voice. Sometimes love's patience *does* know an end. Just ask the wife whose husband has repeatedly cheated on her. Will there not come a day when she pleads for the very last time?

But would you like to know what really has incensed the Savior's heart in this scene? *The Desire of Ages* makes it clear enough. Here is a description of Christ's *first* cleansing of the temple, but Ellen White assures us that by the time of the second cleansing, "the condition of things was even worse than before" (p. 589):

> There came to this feast those who were suffering, those who were in want and distress. The blind, the lame, the deaf, were there. Some were brought on beds. Many came who were too poor to purchase the humblest offering for the Lord, too poor even to buy food with which to satisfy their own hunger. These were greatly distressed by the statements of the priests. The priests boasted of their piety; they claimed to be the guardians of the

people; but they were without sympathy or compassion. The poor, the sick, the dying, made their vain plea for favor. Their suffering awakened no pity in the hearts of the priests (p. 157).

Christ's anger is visibly ignited when the guardians of God's truth spurn the economically disenfranchised, the socially alienated, and the nationally marginalized. The poor, the suffering, the handicapped, and the children—written off by the orthodox. It is the treatment of these by those in positions of leadership and authority that brings down the hot wrath of "gentle Jesus, meek and mild."

Mark it down and mark it well. Here we find orthodoxy *without* orthopraxy. Guardians of the sacred oracles and inspired writings, these religious leaders have all the right knowledge—but without the right practice! They have the *day* of worship right, but they are wrong, dead wrong, about the *way* of worship. The words Jesus quoted as He cleansed the temple—"My house will be called a house of prayer for all nations"— occur in Isaiah 56:7, just two chapters before Isaiah 58. Orthodoxy *without* orthopraxy.

What will it be in the next story?

Story Number Two

"Knowing the correct password—saying 'Master, Master,' for instance—isn't going to get you anywhere with me. What is required is serious obedience—*doing* what my Father wills. I can see it now—at the Final Judgment thousands strutting up to me and saying, 'Master, we preached the Message, we bashed the demons, our God-sponsored projects had everyone talking.' And do you know what I am going to say? 'You missed the boat. All you did was use me to make yourselves important. You don't impress me one bit. You're out of here' " (Matthew 7:21-23 *The Message*, emphasis in original).

Which way does the needle swing in this short story? In the opposite direction from the previous story, that's for sure. Here are a people who have their orthopraxy down pat, but who have totally missed God's required orthodoxy. "You missed the boat." It could be they have the *way* of worship right—but they're wrong, dead wrong, about the *day* of worship.

Orthopraxy *without* orthodoxy. Orthodoxy *without* orthopraxy. Neither combination will get you into heaven, will it? So what will?

Story Number Three

One more story to share. As it turns out, it is the very last story Jesus ever told. And everyone knows that what a dying man saves for last is the most important of all.

"When he finally arrives, blazing in beauty and all his angels with him, the Son of Man will take his place on his glorious throne. Then all the nations will be arranged before him and he will sort the people out, much as a shepherd sorts out sheep and goats, putting sheep to his right and goats to his left.

"Then the King will say to those on his right, 'Enter, you who are blessed by my Father! Take what's coming to you in this kingdom. It's been ready for you since the world's foundation. And here's why:

I was hungry and you fed me,
I was thirsty and you gave me a drink,
I was homeless and you gave me a room,
I was shivering and you gave me clothes,
I was sick and you stopped to visit,
I was in prison and you came to me.'

"Then those 'sheep' are going to say, 'Master, what are you talking about? When did we ever see you hungry and feed you, thirsty and give you a drink? And when did we ever see you sick or in prison and come to you?' Then the King will say, 'I'm telling the solemn truth: Whenever you did one of these things to someone overlooked or ignored, that was me—you did it to me.'

"Then he will turn to the 'goats,' the ones on his left, and say, 'Get out, worthless goats! You're good for nothing but the fires of hell. And why? Because—

I was hungry and you gave me no meal,
I was thirsty and you gave me no drink,
I was homeless and you gave me no bed,
I was shivering and you gave me no clothes,
Sick and in prison, and you never visited.'

"Then those 'goats' are going to say, 'Master, what are you talking about? When did we ever see you hungry or thirsty or homeless or shivering or sick or in prison and didn't help?'

"He will answer them, 'I'm telling the solemn truth: Whenever you failed to do one of these things to someone who was being overlooked or ignored, that was me—you failed to do it to me.'

"Then those 'goats' will be herded to their eternal doom, but the 'sheep' to their eternal reward" (Matthew 25:31-46, *The Message*).

What a bombshell story Jesus saves for His very last one! And which way does He have the needle turning? Without question, here is a story of orthopraxy *superceding* orthodoxy. In fact there is not a single word about "right believing." The entire parable is devoted to defining "right behaving." Right behavior supercedes right belief— would you agree?

The Desire of Ages does. It contains one of the most profound statements regarding the final judgment I have ever read. It's impossible to miss its point:

Thus Christ on the Mount of Olives pictured to His disciples the scene of the great judgment day. And He represented *its decision as turning upon one point*. When the nations are gathered before Him, there will be but two classes, and their eternal destiny will be determined by *what they have done or have ne-*

glected to do for Him in the person of the poor and the suffering (*The Desire of Ages*, p. 637, emphasis supplied).

Did you catch that? On the Judgment Day, the compelling question that Jesus will ask every human being will be *"What did you do for those less fortunate than you?"* When you and I stand before the divine bar of justice, Jesus will not ask us, "What did you believe?" Instead, He will ask us (and every human being) "How did you behave? *What did you do for those less fortunate than you?"* The King will thunder, "The economically disenfranchised, the socially marginalized—the poor and the suffering—I was in them. And what did you do for Me in them and for them in Me?"

Is this a judgment based on orthodoxy? No. The great assize will be based upon orthopraxy. The defining question will not be, "Did you *know* the truth?" Rather, it will be, "Did you *show* the truth?" Orthopraxy *over* orthodoxy, because in the end, the very end, right behavior *supercedes* right belief.[1] We have Jesus' last word on it.

A Fourth Story

But Isaiah 58 offers a fourth story that we must also ponder, along with these three.

Once upon a time there was a chosen people whom God called, "My people," a people who believed they were the champions of orthodoxy. And so they repeated the prophecies. They recited the laws. They remembered the holy day. But they couldn't understand why God was not blessing them as He should, as He had promised.

And so this people of God went to God. They were both flustered and frustrated—or as our daughter Kristin used to say as a child, "I'm fruzzerated, Daddy!" Well, "fruzzerated" they certainly were with their Father. "Why, dear God, are You not blessing us?" they cried out. "Look at how *passionate* we are about You! We worship; we pray; we fast. Good God, we are the champions of *Your* orthodoxy. But still You do not bless us."

And behold (as the story goes), the Lord God in heaven laughed . . . and cried at the same time. For it was true—He *had* asked them to repeat His prophecies and recite His laws and remember His holy day. But from the very beginning He had always hoped that when they championed His orthodoxy, they would champion His orthopraxy as well. For how can there be genuine orthodoxy without orthopraxy? And how can there be genuine orthopraxy without orthodoxy?

And so God laughed. And wept. And was very angry, as heartbroken gods and lovers can be. "You worship me with your lips," He cried in reply, "but you wander far from me with your lives."

> "Shout it aloud, do not hold back.
> > Raise your voice like a trumpet.
> Declare to my people their rebellion
> > and to the house of Jacob their sins.
> For day after day they seek me out;
> > they seem eager to know my ways [orthodoxy],
> as if they were a nation that does what is right [orthopraxy]
> > and has not forsaken the commands of its God.
> They ask me for just decisions
> > and seem eager for God to come near them.
> 'Why have we fasted [been passionate],' they say,
> > 'and you have not seen it?
> Why have we humbled ourselves,
> > and you have not noticed?'

> "Yet on the day of your fasting, you do as you please
> > and exploit all your workers.
> Your fasting ends in quarreling and strife,
> > and in striking each other with wicked fists.
> You cannot fast as you do today
> > and expect your voice to be heard on high.
> Is this the kind of fast [passion] I have chosen,
> > only a day for a man to humble himself?

Is it only for bowing one's head like a reed
>and for lying on sackcloth and ashes?
Is that what you call a fast [being passionate],
>a day acceptable to the LORD?" (Isaiah 58:1-5).

Surely God isn't down on our passion or our orthodoxy, is He? That can't be it. After all, look at how passionate He gets in all four of these stories. But passionate beliefs (orthodoxy) unaccompanied by passionate behavior (orthopraxy) are awfully hollow, aren't they? This fourth story only affirms the previous three. "Do you want to prove you're passionate about Me?" God asks. "Then get off your fasts and embrace My passion!"

And what is God's passion?

In answer God now launches (with great passion) into the very heart and soul of what lies between the bookends:

"Is not this the kind of fasting [passion] I have chosen:
to loose the chains of injustice
>and untie the cords of the yoke,
to set the oppressed free
>and break every yoke?
Is it not to share your food with the hungry
>and to provide the poor wanderer with shelter—
when you see the naked, to clothe him,
>and not to turn away from your own flesh and
blood? . . .

"If you do away with the yoke of oppression,
>with the pointing finger and malicious talk,
and if you spend yourselves in behalf of the hungry
>and satisfy the needs of the oppressed,
then your light will rise in the darkness,
>and your night will become like the noonday" (Isaiah
58:6, 7, 9, 10).

Which being interpreted means: Your orthopraxy (right behavior) must become as passionate as your orthodoxy (right beliefs).

How?

Choose the passion God has chosen. " 'Is this not the kind of fasting [passion] I have chosen?' " And with that God plunges into a checklist of compassion. That is correct—God measures passion by compassion. (Have you ever noticed how similar the words are?)

Compassion for whom?

Did you pick up on how closely Jesus' parable of the sheep and the goats tracks the very same categories of alienated and marginalized human beings that are listed here in Isaiah 58? The hungry, the poor, the naked, the homeless, the imprisoned—the very people we'll be asked about in the final judgment—are the ones God inserts between His bookends here in Isaiah 58.

And what will we be asked? *Did you have* com*passion for 'the least of these' brothers and sisters of Mine?"*

Old Testament, New Testament—God the Father, God the Son—it really doesn't matter, does it? For wherever we turn in sacred Scripture we keep bumping into the same passionately compassionate God. The God who unequivocally declares that *the passion of orthodoxy must be wedded to the compassion of orthopraxy.* "I know you have the bookends down pat," He intones, "but what on earth and what under heaven are you doing for those less fortunate than you?"

It's one of the most stunning truths about God in all of Holy Scripture: He lives night and day in solidarity with the poor! Reading the Scriptures through, I have been astounded to observe how God's incessant and insistent solidarity with the poor is woven into the very fabric of the sacred story.

Viv Grigg, a New Zealander, felt so compelled by God's solidarity with the poor that he moved from the mountain majesty of his South Pacific homeland into the decaying heart of one of Manila's cardboard-and-tin slum cities. I've read his two books, *Companion to the Poor* and *Cry of the Urban Poor,* and I'm moved by the incarnational ministry this one man has undertaken for God.

One day, beneath the corrugated tin roof of his slum house in that Manila *barrio*, Viv sat with a friend and copied by hand onto small white cards every verse in the Bible he could find dealing with the poor. For the next four years he carried them with him, as day and night he meditated upon God's unabashed, uncompromising solidarity with the poor. I wonder what would happen were you and I to meditate on these same texts.

In the English Scriptures, Viv Grigg identified 245 references to the poor, the needy, and poverty. Here is just a handful:

From what is one of the oldest, if not *the* oldest, book in the Bible:

- " 'I rescued the poor who cried for help,
    and the fatherless who had none to assist him.
  The man who was dying blessed me;
    I made the widow's heart sing.
  I put on righteousness as my clothing;
    justice was my robe and my turban.
  I was eyes to the blind
    and feet to the lame.
  I was a father to the needy;
    I took up the case of the stranger' " (Job 29:12-16).
- " 'Have I not wept for those in trouble? Has not my soul grieved for the poor?' " (Job 30:25).

From the very beginning of the community of Israel, God through Moses championed solidarity with the poor:

- "There will always be poor people in the land. Therefore I command you to be openhanded toward your brothers and toward the poor and needy in your land" (Deuteronomy 15:11).
- " ' "When you reap the harvest of your land, do not reap to the very edges of your field or gather the gleanings of your harvest. Do not go over your vineyard a second time or pick up the grapes that have fallen. Leave them for the poor and the alien. I am the LORD your God" ' " (Leviticus 19:9, 10).

Listen to God's solidarity with the poor through the proverbs of wise King Solomon:

- "When you give to the poor, it is like lending to the LORD, and the LORD will pay you back" (Proverbs 19:17, TEV).
- "If you make fun of poor people, you insult the God who made them" (Proverbs 17:5 TEV).
- "He who oppresses the poor shows contempt for their Maker, but whoever is kind to the needy honors God" (Proverbs 14:31).

And the New Testament only continues this tradition of solidarity:

- "Religion that God our Father accepts as pure and faultless is this: to look after orphans and widows in their distress and to keep oneself from being polluted by the world. . . . Listen, my dear brothers: Has not God chosen those who are poor in the eyes of the world to be rich in faith and to inherit the kingdom he promised those who love him?" (James 1:27; 2:5).
- "There were no needy persons among them. For from time to time those who owned lands or houses sold them, brought the money from the sales and put it at the apostles' feet, and it was distributed to anyone as he had need" (Acts 4:34, 35).
- "James, Peter and John, those reputed to be pillars, gave me and Barnabas the right hand of fellowship when they recognized the grace given to me. They agreed that we should go to the Gentiles, and they to the Jews. All they asked was that we should continue to remember the poor, the very thing I was eager to do" (Galatians 2:9, 10).

There they are, just a sample, a handful, of Viv Grigg's 245 Bible statements about the poor, the needy, and poverty. But even from this smattering it is pointedly clear that the Scriptures champion God's unrelenting solidarity with the oppressed, the hungry, the poor, the naked.

Major and minor prophet and apostle alike summon us to share in that solidarity.

And so does Jesus. For without question the most compelling proof of God's solidarity and community with poor people is in the life of the incarnate God Himself. In the words of Viv Grigg, Jesus chose "nondestitute poverty as a way of life" (*Cry of the Urban Poor,* p. 15). Born in a box for cow feed, dead on petty thief's cross, Jesus' sole estate was His underwear and a one-piece tunic over which the grubby soldiers gambled. " 'Foxes have holes and birds of the air have nests, but the Son of Man has no place to lay his head' " (Matthew 8:20).

Conrad Boemer in *The Rich, The Poor—and the Bible* writes:

> The founder of Christianity was himself poor. His identification with others was unprecedented. He gave himself up for the new community. The church is built on his self-surrender. He can be criticized in almost every respect, for his origin, his status, his pretensions, but one thing is irrefutable: his solidarity. Jesus is the embodiment of the poor man (p. 70).

And how deep is His solidarity with the poor, this One who became "the embodiment of the poor man?" He says, "Inasmuch as you have done it to the least of these, My brothers and My sisters—the hungry, the poor, the naked, the sick, the imprisoned—you have done it to Me."

God's most eloquent appeal to us it bound up in the dusty loin cloth of Jesus' utter solidarity with the poor.

> Where can Jesus be found and known today? To find him, we must go where he is. Did he not say, "Where I am, there shall my servant be also"?
>
> *Such a search invariably leads us into the heart of poverty.* For Jesus always goes to the point of deepest need. Where there is suffering, he will be there binding wounds. His compassion eternally drives him to human need. Where there is injustice, he is

there. His justice demands it. He does not dwell on the edge of issues. He is involved, always doing battle with the fiercest of the forces of evil and powers of darkness.

That night, in a squatter settlement . . . my heart found rest. There could be no turning back from God's call. I must preach the gospel to the poor (Viv Grigg, *Companion to the Poor*, p. 22, emphasis supplied).

That is how Viv Grigg responded to God's solidarity with the poor. And how shall we respond—you and I—in our pleasingly middle-class affluence? No *barrios* or slum cities for us. Just the well-manicured comfort of our homey suburban accouterments. Perhaps we're within driving distance of an impoverished inner city, but thank God we're far enough away to enjoy our lovely excesses without having to be constantly reminded of how those "po' folk" live!

Champions of the truth? There isn't an orthodox Adventist whose self-identity believes otherwise. But perhaps it will yet dawn upon us that what God is so agitated about in Isaiah 58 is that *we are poor champions indeed until we champion the poor!*

---

[1] We will return to this parable and its pointed conclusion in the next chapter. Many of us have grown up in and have been educated by a deeply convictional religious community in which the understanding of truth and the advocacy of theological belief hold dominant sway. Hence it is only natural that we would challenge the assertion that orthopraxy supercedes orthodoxy.

CHAPTER THREE

THE CHAMPION

Here in Berrien Springs, Michigan, we're fortunate enough to share our little village with one of the most famous living sports heroes on earth, Mohammed Ali. Years ago, when I was a seminary student here at Andrews University, the buzz around campus was that Mohammed Ali had moved into town and was opening his boxing training sessions to the public. So we students flocked down to that renovated barn at the end of Kephart Street to watch "the Champ" display his nimble prowess. This was in the days when Ali could still "float like a butterfly, sting like a bee"— before he was infected with Parkinson's disease.

The boxing ring was in the center of the old barn. Pinned up along the top of all four walls were full-color magazine covers from around the world, featuring that famous grinning visage of the world's heavyweight boxing champion. "I am the greatest!" several magazine cover headlines proclaimed.

The afternoon I showed up in that crowded barn, Ali was at his spry best. He nimbly danced around the ring, jabbing at his sparring partner, ducking the return punches. And all the while he was carrying on a lively banter with the crowd of us students. Then, for some inexplicable reason, one of the students began to taunt the Champ. I looked across the ring at the kid, aghast that anybody would dare take on this heavyweight. Ali fired a verbal punch back at the student, but the young man was unintimidated, and he shot back another quip. To which Ali yelled out another retort over his sweaty shoulder as he kept sparring. (Clearly, Ali was enjoying the verbal match.) That went on for a few more moments, when suddenly Ali darted away from his training partner and with his massive gloved forearm high in the air lunged toward the kid! I was nearly passing out from vicarious fright as the world heavyweight boxing champion swung his giant fist toward the student on the other side of the ropes. And I tell you the truth, to the accompanying sounds of a horrified collective gasp, Ali missed that boy's nose by a few millimeters.

As it turned out, it had all been an act! And once we recovered from our spent adrenalin, everybody cheered the Champ!

The world loves a champion. So does God, which is why He came to earth to be one. And though He never went about declaring, "I am the greatest!" it is unarguably clear that He became the greatest Champion of all time on behalf of a very particular demographic slice of His earth children.

Strap on your seat belt, and let's fly through an entire Gospel in one very brief sitting, pausing only to connect the dots. But when the dots are all connected, we will see a sketched portrait (albeit a rough one) of the Champion as perhaps you've never seen Him before.

Which Gospel shall we choose? More than any other Gospel writer, Dr. Luke, the lone Gentile writer in the New Testament, champions Jesus' solidarity with the poor. For that reason Luke has been a favorite Gospel of the radical liberation theologians in Central and South America. And for the same reason it is essential we link Isaiah 58's impassioned appeal to social justice and social action to Luke's compelling defense of the poor. So with Luke as our focus, let's fly. Let's look at Jesus' solidarity with the poor in Luke's Gospel.

- *Intimations of His solidarity—1:53.* Here the young virgin Mary sings of her trust in God to fulfill the promise of the angel that she would give birth to the Son of the Most High. And here in this teenager's song is the line, "He has filled the hungry with good things but has sent the rich away empty." Here are intimations even before He was even born that Jesus would take up the cause of the hungry and poor.

- *Born into solidarity—Luke 2:7, 15, 24.* These are the familiar Christmas texts that sketch the crude backyard cave into which the Christ Child was born, His crib a box of cow feed, born into poverty, this One who would become the poor's Champion. So poor were His parents, in fact, that they could bring to the temple only the minimal liturgical offering proscribed for the impoverished, " 'a pair of doves or two young pigeons' " (see Leviticus 12:8).

- *Inaugural solidarity—Luke 4:17-19.* Flying over childhood and young adulthood, Luke hurries us next to a front-row seat for Jesus' inaugural hometown sermon, exclusively recorded in this Gospel. Excited to have the hometown Boy back in Nazareth, the worship leader that Sabbath handed Jesus the scroll for Isaiah and invited Him to address the congregation. Luke carefully describes what happened next:

Unrolling it, he found the place where it is written:

"The Spirit of the Lord is on me,

    because he has anointed me to preach good news to the poor.

He has sent me to proclaim freedom for the prisoners

    and recovery of sight for the blind,

to release the oppressed,

    to proclaim the year of the Lord's favor" (Luke 4:17-19).

Note that Jesus personally and carefully selected the passage He would read—no assigned selection would do. And He chose for His reading a passage that dramatically prophesied the Messiah's unequivocal solidarity with the poor, the prisoners, the infirmed, the oppressed—that is, the very categories God passionately identifies in Isaiah 58, the identical categories with which the King in Matthew's judgment parable claims solidarity! Luke will not let us forget that solidarity.

- *Solidarity in the Beatitudes—Luke 6:20, 21, 24, 25.* The solidarity here is so compelling we will return to it in a moment and ponder its radical depths.

- *Lifestyle of solidarity—Luke 9:57, 58; 10:4, 7.* Here Luke records the well-known retort of Jesus to an eager prospective disciple who hoped to hitch his star to Jesus' wagon: " 'Foxes have holes and birds of the air have nests, but the Son of Man has no place to lay his head' " (Luke 9:58). In other words, "The wagon you want to hitch up to doesn't even have a garage," Jesus told him. The young adult Messiah has clearly renounced middle-class security in favor of solidarity with the homeless. For that reason, before sending His disciples out on a missionary visit, Jesus instructs them to forget about taking any currency along (who has any, anyway?) and to plan, instead, on staying wherever they could find a hospitable home that would board them. Such is the life of the homeless Jesus.
- *Parable of solidarity—Luke 10:36, 37.* Everybody loves the Good Samaritan story. Its inescapable punch line is a rather impassioned appeal to see every human being in need as our neighbor. The victim at the side of the road may not have been a poor man, but he certainly was in a poor and pitiful state. The hero of Jesus' story is the one who inconveniences himself on behalf of the poor suffering one. Solidarity with the needy, indeed!
- *Parable of antisolidarity—Luke 12:15-21, 33.* Luke sketches Jesus' portrait as Champion of the poor using reverse strokes as well, as he does in recording Jesus telling a withering parable *against* a rich land owner. We remember Christ's antihero as "the rich fool," since in His story that is what Jesus has God calling the wealthy farmer: "You fool!" (verse 20). Of course, the poor among Luke's Gentile readers would find particular comfort in noting death's great reversal of the rich man's fortunes. And then, a few paces beyond that parable, Luke records the words of Christ: " 'Sell your possessions and give to the poor. Provide purses for yourselves that will not wear out, a treasure in heaven that will not be exhausted, where no thief comes near and no moth destroys' " (Luke 12:33). Solidarity with the poor—you can't miss it.

- *Call for solidarity—Luke 14:13, 21.* It's not your typical list for a wedding or dinner invitation, but Luke twice makes certain we know that when Jesus thinks of having a party He makes sure His list includes "the poor, the crippled, the lame, the blind" (Luke 14:13, 21). These are the kind of people the Champion invites His followers to embrace.

- *Antisolidarity among the religious—Luke 16:13, 14.* Jesus' strong bias against the love of riches and His proclivity toward the poor is further sketched across Luke's canvas with the observation: "The Pharisees, who loved money, heard all this and were sneering at Jesus" (Luke 16:14). Obviously, not everyone in the church will be excited about our Champion's solidarity with the poor.

- *Antisolidarity among the rich—Luke 16:19-31.* Luke alone records Jesus' parable of the rich man and the poor beggar Lazarus. Surely the poor among Luke's readers would find no small comfort in this tale that taught that death would yet right the economic wrongs of this life and reverse the monetary inequities of this earthly existence. With a heart for the poor, Jesus tells a story that declares the impoverished will not forever be so! Divine judgment after death will settle the score and right the wrongs.

- *Solidarity as a choice—Luke 18:22; 19:8.* It is no accident that Luke places two very familiar stories—the story of the rich young ruler and the story of Zacchaeus, the tax collector—in close proximity. The rich young ruler, who had it all, mournfully walked away from Jesus' invitation to sell it all and give it to the poor so that he could follow Jesus. "How hard," Jesus somberly confessed, "it is for the rich to enter the kingdom of God!" Hard, yes—impossible, no. For Luke follows with the glad story of the short, little tax collector, Zacchaeus, as rich, himself, as the rich young ruler. But what a dramatic contrast in endings! For without any prompting and from humble gratitude for the Savior's love, Zacchaeus blurts out that he will give half his possessions to the poor. Solidarity with the poor—the rich young ruler rejected it, but not so the short, saved tax collector.

- *Commendation of solidarity—Luke 21:1-4.* Jesus' loud stage whisper in the temple courtyard sent a very poor widow home from church with a heart bursting with gratitude. How would you like to come to church, place an offering in the plate, and have the preacher stand up and announce that poor little you have just given more than all the rich people in church that morning combined! Solidarity with the poor—Jesus commended it in all who would follow Him.

- *Solidarity in death—Luke 23:43.* You generally don't become a thief because you're rich. Usually it's because you're poor, dirt poor, that you resort to robbery. How did the Champion of the poor die? He was nailed up between two poor convicted thieves. Jesus demonstrated His solidarity with the poor even in death. But because one of those poor men reached out in faith to the dying Champion, Jesus craned his neck sideways just so that He might assure the poor thief that their solidarity would continue one day in Paradise. To the end, Christ was one with the poor, wasn't He?

- *Buried and resurrected in solidarity—Luke 23:50-53.* Luke keeps sketching the Champion's solidarity with the poor right through His death and into His burial and resurrection. In this case, Luke maintains that solidarity by omitting what Matthew made sure we all would know—that the man who buried Jesus was rich (see Matthew 27:57). In Luke, we find not a word of Joseph of Arimathea's wealth because for Luke, Jesus is the Champion of the poor. And that's the way Luke wanted to leave it in the very last parchment of his Gospel. The One who died, was buried, and rose again—who is He? Luke, more than any other writer, exclaims, "He is the Champion of the poor!"

There it is—compelling historical testimony of Jesus' solidarity with the poor. In Him, they found an unrelenting Advocate and Friend—not only in word, but also in deed, not only in admonition, but also in example. Luke's conclusion is plain to see: The poor Man is our Friend.

It makes you wonder, doesn't it, if we, as His followers, are supposed to "go and do likewise" (Luke 10:37), as He put it after the parable of the Good Samaritan. Liberation theologians declare without hesitation that the answer is, "Yes." Clodovis Boff and George V. Pixley, in their book *The Bible, the Church, and the Poor,* have concluded: "Following Jesus demands solidarity with the poor, service to the needs of the humblest, and readiness to suffer persecution that will follow from these actions" (p. 71).

But if liberation theologians aren't your cup of tea, then how about considering the conclusion of another writer who also championed the poor a century ago:

> Christ's chief work was in ministering to the poor, the needy, and the ignorant. In simplicity He opened before them the blessings they might receive, and thus aroused a soul hunger for the bread of life. *Christ's life is an example to all His followers* (Ellen White, *Welfare Ministry,* p. 59, emphasis supplied).

The unavoidable, "unduckable," inescapable question, therefore, is simple: *"Is Christ's life an example to us, too, in the third millennium of Christianity?"*

Well, you may be thinking, *perhaps the needs are not as great today as they were in the time of Christ.* Come again? *TIME* magazine published a feature story entitled "The Real Face of Homelessness" (January 20, 2003, pp. 52-61). Here are some statistics from that article that need to catch our hearts as well as our eyes:

- The U.S. Conference of Mayors conducted a survey in which they discovered that demand for homeless shelters spiked 13 percent since the previous December.
- Our nation is experiencing subtle changes in the complexion of the homeless population. In contrast to our usual conception of the homeless as the hardcore unemployed, now one in five resi-

dents of homeless shelters holds a full- or part-time job. (These people—waiters, security guards, laborers, and other low-paid workers—once earned enough to pay their rent but have been squeezed between high housing costs and stagnant wages.)

- Families are now the fastest growing segment of homeless.
- Numbers indicate that for the fourth year in a row there is no jurisdiction in the United States (except Puerto Rico) where a person on minimum wage can afford to rent a one-bedroom home at fair market value.
- *TIME* calls these new homeless, "the working poor on a losing streak."

Consider the observations of Janice Wrenn, a professor in the Social Work Department at Andrews University, who analyzes our national poverty in a book edited by Herb Helm, a psychologist in the Behavioral Sciences Department of this same university:

> Millions of Americans with full-time working family members are poor. Being employed does not guarantee escape from poverty. In the mid 1990s, the working poor were almost equally distributed among cities, suburbs, and rural areas. Most (62%) had graduated from high school, most were White, and about half were married (Herb Helm, ed., *Many Voices: An Introduction to Social Issues,* p. 236).

After a recent worship service in which we considered Isaiah 58's rather radical call to solidarity with the poor, two worshipers came up to me separately after the service and remarked that many of the poor are free-loaders who are not willing to work hard and thus extricate themselves from poverty. Janice Wrenn's essay challenges that notion:

> Some argue that the working poor are lazy and that if they worked harder and longer they would not be poor. However, studies have shown that most of the working poor would re-

main poor even if they worked 40 hours a week, 52 weeks a year. Thus, working more hours is not a solution to poverty because the problem is low wages or jobs that do not provide full-time employment. . . . At the end of the 1990s, a minimum wage earner, paid $5.15 per hour, would earn $10,300 per year. This is far below the $16,660 poverty threshold of four (ibid.).

What did *TIME* magazine call them? "The working poor on a losing streak." They are impoverished Americans who earn just enough to be ineligible for most assistance programs. Shall we berate them for their laziness or castigate them for their lack of frugality? A recent *Parade* magazine cover story—"How Can We Help End Childhood Hunger"—carried this alarming statistic:

Last year, according to the Department of Agriculture, 34.9 million Americans . . . were "food insecure"—the government's term for those who must survive on a diet not nutritious enough to keep a child healthy. More than 13 million of those people were children. The U.S. Conference of Mayors expects that requests for emergency food from families with children will increase in 91% of the nation's cities this year. They also document that emergency food outlets in 56% of the nation's cities turned away hungry families last year because they ran out of resources (*Parade,* April 4, 2004, p. 6).

Will it really ease our consciences to suggest that if the poor would just work harder and scrimp more, they could make it? Oscar Wilde once quipped, "To recommend thrift to the poor is both grotesque and insulting. It is like advising a man who is starving to eat less."

So what would Jesus have us to do?

The media have poked fun at a Christian group out of Pennsylvania that has been advocating that when it comes to gas-guzzling SUVs, we need to ask the question, "What would Jesus do?" Their conclusion: He wouldn't drive one. And while I've been amused at the defensive responses of some Christians (no doubt SUV drivers) who have labored to argue that because He had twelve disciples, Jesus would surely have needed a big SUV just to haul His troop around, nevertheless the Pennsylvania group's point is well taken. What *would* Jesus do?

Or more specifically, What would Jesus do for the poor of our community and county and country *were He in your shoes and mine?* Didn't we just read: "Christ's chief work was in ministering to the poor, the needy, and the ignorant. . . . Christ's life is an example to all His followers" (*Welfare Ministry*, p. 59)? Doesn't that mean it is entirely appropriate to be asking what He would do?

Let's return for a moment to the solidarity segment we skipped over earlier as we were surveying Luke's portrayal of Jesus—the Sermon on the Mount. How radically different is Luke's telling of this sermon from Matthew's account! Jesus' unapologetic championing of the poor is inescapable here in Luke:

> Looking at his disciples, he said:
> "Blessed are you who are poor,
> for yours is the kingdom of God.
> Blessed are you who hunger now,
>   for you will be satisfied. . . .
> But woe to you who are rich,
>   for you have already received your comfort.
> Woe to you who are well fed now,
>   for you will go hungry" (Luke 6:20, 21, 24, 25).

What's up with this dramatic, almost "in-your-face" contrast between Jesus' attitude to the poor and His attitude to the rich? Matthew smoothes Jesus' words over to simply read, " 'Blessed are the poor in spirit' " (Matthew 5:3). But for Luke, who champions the poor as does Jesus, it is, "Blessed are the poor." And then Luke, unlike Matthew, goes on to add the woe Jesus pronounces against the rich. What's up with that?

Let's get one thing straight—Jesus is *not* down on rich people. The rich are recipients of God's grace just as much as are the poor. Some of Jesus' "best friends" were rich—Nicodemus, Zacchaeus, Abraham, and Solomon. And the rabble (the poor and impoverished) were the ones screaming for His blood at the end. So, it isn't a matter of who is friends with whom. Obviously, God loves all His children alike.

However, the compelling issue here in Luke's telling of the Sermon on the Mount is human selfishness. In raw contrast, Jesus draws a distinction between humility and pride. "Blessed are the dirt poor for you have nothing in life left to be proud of, and God one day will give you everything. But woe on the filthy rich for you have everything in life you're proud of, and God one day will leave you nothing."

Jesus is pleading for the hearts of the poor *and* the rich. And in clarion tones, He notes what He would later somberly declare about the rich young ruler—"How hard it is for the rich to enter the kingdom of God!" (Luke 18:24). For it is the needy who are nearest to salvation. After all, what else do they have! "Blessed are you who are poor." While it is true that poverty will save no man or woman, neither will riches. But, clearly, an impoverished life is a shortcut to an impoverished heart. And an impoverished heart is most open to the offer of God. That's why Jesus says, "Blessed are you who are poor."

But because the grip of selfishness is no respecter of persons, rich or poor, Jesus enjoins upon all who would follow Him a solitary passionate appeal just a few lines later: " 'Give to everyone who asks of you' " (Luke 6:30, NKJV). He makes no distinctions here about economic categories or financial accumulations. For the poor or the rich or those in between, the injunction is the same: "Give to everyone who asks of you."

Why? Because nothing cuts to the heart of human selfishness—the spirit of clinging to—more radically than the act of giving—the spirit of letting go. Jesus is clear. If you're poor, then give. If you're rich, then give. If you're middle class, then give. *"Give to everyone who asks of you."*

I wonder what would happen if we followed that injunction. What would happen if we gave *something* for *every* request you and I receive?

To the homeless panhandler by the side of the road, to the ring-a-linging Salvation Army volunteer outside Wal-Mart, to the telemarketing charity caller on the phone, to the sales pitch at the door for tickets to the Firemen's Pancake Breakfast, to the heart-tugging ADRA appeal in the mail, to the pleading desperate pastor in the pulpit (you didn't think I would leave us pastors out, did you?)—"Give to everyone who asks of you."

"But wait a minute," you quickly protest. "How am I to know how genuine the financial needs really are? How can I be sure of these persons' fiduciary honesty? How do I know the money will ever get to that Guatemalan orphan?"

Fair questions, all of them.

But remember what is at stake here. The issue that Jesus is concerned about isn't so much the Firemen's Pancake Breakfast as it is the congenital selfishness of my everyday heart. Jesus doesn't command you or me to give "whatever they ask for." But He does enjoin upon us, "Give to everyone who asks." He doesn't admonish us, "Give all." But He is incontrovertibly clear, "Give to all who ask." He doesn't say how much. He just says, "Give."

And while there are a host of out-stretched hands that come to us through the mail or over the telephone, there is one within our own community of faith that surely deserves our "extra" attention. The Adventist Development and Relief Agency (ADRA) is "our own" 24/7 humanitarian ministry. You and I will never be able to mobilize ourselves or our friends to respond to every global crisis. But ADRA can go; ADRA can minister; ADRA can take the compassionate touch of Jesus to the hungry, the thirsty, the suffering, the poor, the victims. Whether in the famine-stricken Sudan or hurricane-ravaged Tuscaloosa or war-scarred Kosovo, you and I can hurry to the side of the next round of earth's victims through our financial support of ADRA's global mission.[1]

Why? Because Jesus said, "Give to everyone who asks." He's gunning for our hearts, not our wallets. It's the clutching, choking grip of our own selfishness that Christ seeks to loosen. The sad reality of our earthy humanity is that if God cannot loosen that grip, we will literally strangle ourselves to death. Which is why over a century ago this terse line was written: "Continual giving starves covetousness to death" (Ellen White, *Testimonies for the Church,* vol. 3, p. 548).

"Give to everyone who asks of you." According to Jesus, *nothing is so powerful an antidote to selfishness as unselfishness.*

And guess what? The standard by which you give to others will be the standard by which you'll receive from God. " 'Give, and it will be given to you. A good measure, pressed down, shaken together and running over, will be poured into your lap. *For with the measure you use, it will be measured to you'* " (Luke 6:38, emphasis supplied). Whether rich or poor, if you live a stingy, selfish life, you'll receive a stingy, selfish verdict in the end.

And it was here that the light bulb suddenly went on in my mind the other day. Remember the parable of the sheep and the goats in Matthew 25 that we looked at in a previous chapter of this book? Remember how King Jesus one day will declare to the righteous, "I was hungry, and you fed Me; naked, and you clothed Me; lonely, and you took Me in; in prison, and you visited Me"? And the saved will cry out, "Impossible! We never saw You—really, we didn't! How could we have ever done that to You?"

But Jesus will answer, "Inasmuch as you did it to one of the least of these My brothers and sisters, you did it to Me" (see Matthew 25:40).

Do you remember, too, how the judgment went against the lost because they did nothing for the poor, the naked, the homeless, the imprisoned—the disenfranchised and alienated and marginalized?

After thinking about Jesus' words in Luke's telling of the Sermon on the Mount, it suddenly hit me what that line from *The Desire of Ages* is trying to tell us:

> Thus Christ on the Mount of Olives pictured to His disciples the scene of the great judgment day. And He represented its decision as turning upon one point. When the nations are gathered before Him, there will be but two classes, and their

eternal destiny will be determined by what they have done or have neglected to do for Him in the person of the poor and the suffering (*The Desire of Ages*, p. 637).

Why will the judgment turn on how we treated the poor in this life? Because nothing cuts more quickly or deeply to the core of human selfishness or unselfishness than our response to the plight of those in need. Is there a more visible barometer of the condition of my heart than my response to the needs of the poor around me? Lucifer's original sin, I remind you, was a strangulating pride and selfishness. What more visible or verifiable standard of judgment could there be than to measure the presence or absence of selfishness in us on the basis of how we responded in this life to the needy around us?

The rich young ruler stood for a fleeting moment before God's judgment bar as Jesus gave him the shining opportunity to prove his professed love and loyalty to God by liquidating his other gods and giving the proceeds to the poor. Jesus knew then what He will know in the judgment, which is that a mere profession of love to God will not suffice. There must be a tangible visible standard whereby all will know the depth of the lips' confession. Which is why Jesus' command to the rich young ruler will be His query in the final judgment: "The poor, the poor, the poor—what did you do for them?"

No wonder John exclaims: "Those who say, 'I love God,' and hate their brothers or sisters, are liars; for those who do not love a brother or sister whom they have seen, cannot love God whom they have not seen" (1 John 4:20, NRSV).

In the judgment Jesus will be clear: "Inasmuch as you did it, or did not do it, for those brothers and sisters in need—you did it, or did not do it, for Me." That certainly uncomplicates the judgment, doesn't it? Because nobody will have to read the mind or heart then. The life we lived on this earth—how we treated those less fortunate than we were—will be evidence enough where our hearts really were. That could mean that Mother Teresa may get in—and you and I may not! Because to repeat our previous discovery, orthopraxy will indeed supercede orthodoxy. Or as James put it: "Judgment without mercy will be shown to anyone who has not been merciful. *Mercy triumphs over judgment!*" (James 2:13, emphasis supplied).

That is why God is so passionate in our theme chapter, Isaiah 58. "You have the bookends of the Sabbath and the sanctuary," He cries out, "but where is what lies between? Where is your social justice? Where is your social action? Where are your hearts?"

> . . . I want you to share your food with the hungry and to welcome poor wanderers into your homes. Give clothes to those who need them, and do not hide from relatives who need your help.
>
> If you do these things, your salvation will come like the dawn. Yes, your healing will come quickly. Your godliness will lead you forward, and the glory of the LORD will protect you from behind" (Isaiah 58:7, 8, NLT).

Apparently God knows that *nothing is so powerful an antidote to selfishness as unselfishness.* And just as apparently, nothing can help us become unselfish more effectively than giving to the poor. For with the measure you give to others in this life, God will give to you in the judgment. So "give to everyone who asks of you."

Thus says the Champion of the poor, who once upon a time incarnated Himself among the poor so that we might find Him there. Maybe it is time we started looking for Him among the poor.

Mother Teresa once told a rich American visitor who couldn't comprehend "her fierce commitment to the dregs of Calcutta," as Philip Yancey puts it in his book, *The Jesus I Never Knew* (p. 233): "We are a contemplative order. First we meditate on Jesus, and then we go out and look for him in disguise."

---

[1] For information on how to become a partner in ADRA's humanitarian mission, go to its website: www.ADRA.org.

CHAPTER FOUR

Trapped in the Spin Cycle

A six-year-old girl in Long Beach, California, accompanied her mother and siblings to a nearby laundromat. While mother was loading the washers, the kids decided to play hide-and-seek. As her siblings counted with their eyes closed, the girl searched the laundromat for a suitable hiding place. In a flash she spotted one. While her mother was distracted, she climbed into one of the front-loading washers and closed the door behind her. Nobody would be able to find her now.

The unsuspecting mother walked down the line of washers, depositing quarters to begin the cycle on each machine. When the quarters dropped in, an automatic electronic lock bolted each washer door shut. When the hot water began spraying into the washer, the little girl in hiding quickly concluded it was time to get out! But when she tried to push the door open, she discovered it was firmly locked!

Panic! And pounding! In a flash mother and children spotted her petrified face pressed against the glass door window. Desperately her mother pulled and tugged against the locked washer door to no avail. The water inside was rising. In near panic herself, her mother ran out into the street screaming for help. A motorist slammed to a stop. Hurrying into the laundromat, he tried pulling the door open. But the lock held; the water was still rising. Racing back out to his car for a tire iron, the young man returned and smashed the glass window, reached inside the washer and dragged the young girl out just in time. The child underwent surgery for lacerations to her face and body. Her rescuer received stitches to his arm and was released. The end.[1]

But for the poor the story doesn't usually end with a rescue, does it? Too often stuck in circumstances beyond their control, locked into their impoverished economic state, they have no way out. Their only hope is that someone might notice their plight and rescue them.

And that is God's hope, too:

> "Is not this the kind of fasting I have chosen:
> to loose the chains of injustice
>   and untie the cords of the yoke,
> to set the oppressed free
>   and break every yoke?
> Is it not to share your food with the hungry
>   and to provide the poor wanderer with shelter—
> when you see the naked, to clothe him,
>   and not to turn away from your own flesh and
> blood?" (Isaiah 58:6, 7).

Did you notice that God's call to solidarity with the poor begins with the words "your own flesh and blood"? That is, your own family. Or your own "Family," with a capital "F." Because let's face it, the poor are not only "out there"; the poor are also "in here"—in our own "Family."

In fact, the Old Testament treatment of God's solidarity with the poor is almost exclusively devoted to the poor *within* the community of faith. Take God's admonition through Moses to the children of Israel, before they moved into the Promised Land:

> But if there are any poor people in your towns when you arrive in the land the LORD your God is giving you, do not be hard-hearted or tightfisted toward them. Instead, be generous and lend them whatever they need. . . . Give freely without begrudging it, and the LORD your God will bless you in every-

thing you do. *There will always be some among you who are poor.* That is why I am commanding you to share your resources freely with the poor and with other Israelites in need (Deuteronomy 15:7, 8, 10, 11, NLT, emphasis supplied).

Centuries later, when Jesus and His disciples were happily reclining about Simon the Pharisee's bountiful dinner table, Jesus quoted this line from Deuteronomy. Mary had just "privately" anointed her Master's feet with some costly perfume, and the air was heavy with its scent. With two sniffs, Judas spotted the act of utterly selfless devotion. The contrast with his own avarice was too painful for him to contain, so he hissed something about how the money ought to have been given to the poor. Poor Judas, who could have cared less about the poor, suddenly is their champion! Jesus smells odoriferous hypocrisy in the air and springs to the defense of Mary's now besmirched devotion. " 'Leave her alone. . . . You will always have the poor among you, but you will not always have me' " (John 12:7, 8).

Both testaments share the same point—the poor we will always have with us. "So what are you going to do for them," God asks in Isaiah 58, "these poor of your own Family?"

Would you like to see what the primitive church did for the poor in the days of its beginning? By the way, in a profile of the new generation of young adults in the church today (the twenty-somethings), Robert Webber (*The Younger Evangelicals: Facing the Challenges of the New World*, p. 54) identifies twenty-four characteristics that define these new "millennials," as they're being called. Among those twenty-four characteristics are these two: (1) they long for community, and (2) they are committed to the plight of the poor, especially in urban centers. It occurs to me that this new post-9/11 generation is a perfect fit for primitive Christianity, because the church in Acts felt the very same way—they were deeply committed to the plight of the poor, and they shared an intense longing for community. Examine the evidence in Acts for yourself:

That day about three thousand took [Peter] at his word, were baptized and were signed up. They committed themselves to the teaching of the apostles, the life together, the common meal, and the prayers. Everyone around was in awe—all those wonders and signs done through the apostles! And all the believers lived in a wonderful harmony, holding everything in common. They sold whatever they owned and pooled their resources so that each person's need was met.

They followed a daily discipline of worship in the Temple followed by meals at home, every meal a celebration, exuberant and joyful, as they praised God. People in general liked what they saw. Every day their number grew as God added those who were saved (Acts 2:41-47, *The Message*).

Don't you dream of a day when that profile of the early Christian church becomes a portrait of us—a snapshot of *every* Seventh-day Adventist congregation in *every* village and city and country of the world? Why couldn't it happen? It surely must be God's dream, too.

And did you notice that in the context of vibrant community "each person's need was met"? The poor were truly cared for. Was this just an aberration, a blip on the radar screen in the beginning? Read on:

The whole congregation of believers was united as one—one heart, one mind! They didn't even claim ownership of their own possessions. No one said, "That's mine; you can't have it." They shared everything. The apostles gave powerful witness to the resurrection of the Master Jesus, and grace was on all of them.

And so it turned out that not a person among them was needy. Those who owned fields or houses sold them and brought the price of the sale to the apostles and made an offering of it. The apostles then distributed it according to each person's need (Acts 4:32-35, *The Message*).

That's quite a testimony for a city congregation, isn't it? "They shared everything." Do you suppose that's what God had in mind in Isaiah 58? Here's another snapshot:

During this time, as the disciples were increasing in numbers by leaps and bounds, hard feelings developed among the Greek-speaking believers—"Hellenists"—toward the Hebrew-speaking believers because their widows were being discriminated against in the daily food lines. So the Twelve called a meeting of the disciples. They said, "It wouldn't be right for us to abandon our responsibilities for preaching and teaching the Word of God to help with the care of the poor. So, friends, choose seven men from among you whom everyone trusts, men full of the Holy Spirit and good sense, and we'll assign them this task. Meanwhile, we'll stick to our assigned tasks of prayer and speaking God's Word (Acts 6:1-5, *The Message*).

Care for the poor wasn't an aberration at all, was it? It was the early church's way of life. Incidentally, the Greek name for "Acts," this book that tells the story of the early church, is *Praxis*. Remember that word? It's in the last half of orthopraxy (right actions, right behaviors). The early Christians certainly had their orthopraxy and their orthodoxy in Christlike balance, did they not?

Now I realize that some Christians are perturbed and disturbed by these accounts in Acts of what clearly is a stunning solidarity with the poor in the very beginning of the church. Naturally protective of their own pocketbooks and wallets and portfolios, these wealthier Christians read what we have just read and worry about a word we don't use much anymore: *egalitarianism*. It means: "of, relating to, or believing in political and social equality."[2]

A vivid example of egalitarian philosophy would be the communism of a generation ago. A year before the Berlin Wall came down, I traveled by subway from West Berlin to East Berlin for part of a day. When I came up out of the subway into East Berlin, I was taken aback by the very evident contrast between the two halves of that one city. The buildings, the street signs, the store fronts, the display windows, the department-store shelves—the composite picture was all so drab and gray and colorless there in communist East Berlin. Communism attempted to level the playing field politically, socially, and economically, resulting in a very dour picture of human life. If this is egalitarianism, you can have it!

Some read Acts and wonder, *Is that what God is calling for—an egalitarian church in which all the wealthy must become poor in order to be saved?* But Acts is hardly advocating such uniformity. Zdravko Plantak has written:

> God the Creator is not egalitarian [everyone forced into economic uniformity and social equality]. To be sure, God made us equal in dignity, equal in value. But God did not make us equal in gifts. Some people He made more intelligent than others; some more handsome than others; some more healthy than others; some are tall, others are not; some are thin, and others are not. He has made us all different. Our doctrine of creation is about an *equality of value* with a *diversity of gifts* (*Adventist Review*, November 2002, p. 29).

What God champions in Holy Scripture, Plantak goes on to note, is "equality of opportunity," equal access to the gospel, "equal access to the good earth," equal access to food, water, health-care, and education (ibid.).

Then the question naturally arises: If God champions equality of opportunity, why does He say the poor will always be with us? The answer must lie somewhere in the reality of our moral and global fallenness. When the system of life collapses—ecologically or economically, militarily or morally—when human nature or Mother Nature itself breaks down, inevitably people are caught in the fall. And poor people are often what is left of the survivors. In a fallen world, "The poor you will always have with you." Such poverty is not the will of God; rather, it is the inevitable condition of humanity in a fallen civilization.

But lest we conclude that the poor are a "perennial and insoluble problem," Plantak reminds us that in Deuteronomy 15 the God who declares, "There will always be poor people in the land" (verse 11), is the same God who seven verses earlier commands, "There should be no poor among you" (verse 4). How shall we resolve that tension? Plantak responds:

There's only one way to reconcile [these two statements]: *There should not be poor,* because poverty is not God's will; *There will continue to be poor,* because of the continuance of human injustice. The will of God says there should not be any poor. Human injustice ensures there'll continue to be poor. Thus the continuing existence of poverty in the world mentioned in Deuteronomy 15 is not as an excuse for inaction, but an argument for generosity (Plantak, p. 28).

And it is that generosity that is the shining hallmark of the New Testament church—a community of faith that championed an "equality of opportunity" for all her children. And "there were no needy persons among them" (Acts 4:34).

So what about the poor in our own midst? God does not globally enforce His kingdom of love and opportunity . . . yet. And so in that "not yetness" many even within our Family still suffer, stuck in the spin cycle of painful poverty.

I knocked on their basement apartment door. I'd heard that the young couple, members of our congregation and students at the university, were experiencing some financial difficulties. And while such stories are hardly unique in a community of young penniless scholars in training, I decided I had better check this one out. It was not long before Christmas. The young husband invited me in. Sitting there in that nearly bare apartment, the three of us fell into conversation. At some point in our visit, I asked how things were going financially for them. They glanced at each other for a moment. Then the young man stood up and walked to their refrigerator and opened it. He pointed at a half-empty tub of butter and a jar of corn kernels. "This is what we've been living on lately." They were subsisting on popcorn. "The poor you will always have with you."

Could it be that the God who tenderly loves those who suffer leaves those who suffer in our midst to see what we will do for them? To confront our selfishness, to grow our characters, to test our love. Could that be it? "The poor you will always have with you."

In a chapter entitled "God's Care for the Poor" is this observation:

There is nothing, after their recognition of the claims of God, that more distinguishes the laws given by Moses than the liberal, tender, and hospitable spirit enjoined toward the poor. Although God had promised greatly to bless His people, it was not His design that poverty should be wholly unknown among them. He declared that the poor should never cease out of the land. *There would ever be those among His people who would call into exercise their sympathy, tenderness, and benevolence.* Then, as now, persons were subject to misfortune, sickness, and loss of property; yet so long as they followed the instruction given by God, there were no beggars among them, neither any who suffered for food (Ellen White, *Patriarchs and Prophets,* pp. 530, 531, emphasis supplied).

"The poor you will always have with you." Given that reality, could it be that *the poor are our golden opportunity to exercise the golden rule?* If the tables were turned and your fortunes reversed, how would you want that poor man, that poor woman, that poor student, that poor child in our midst to treat you? If you were the poor one, locked in poverty's spin cycle from which you were unable to extricate yourself, and she, the poor one, had all your money, your time, and your talents—how would you want her to treat you in your need? " 'So in everything, do to others what you would have them to do to you, for this sums up the Law and the Prophets' " (Matthew 7:12). The poor *in our midst* are our golden opportunity to exercise the golden rule, are they not?

Just like Jesus.

And just like His primitive church in Acts, whose orthopraxy proved their orthodoxy, giving evidence of His generous love to the city and world around them. Wasn't that Jesus' passionate point just before He died? "By this the whole world will know you are My people, if you have love for one another" (see John 13:35). It is His eleventh commandment.[3] "As Christ had loved them, the disciples were to love one another. They were to show forth the love abiding in their hearts for men, women, and children, by doing all in their power for their salvation. *But they were to reveal a specially tender love for all of the same faith*" (Ellen White, MS 160, 1898, emphasis supplied).

"A specially tender love for all of the same faith." That was the explosive secret of the primitive church! Their loving solidarity for each other—poor and rich alike—became their most potent evangelistic strategy. Conrad Boerma is right:

> [In Acts] the mutual solidarity of Christ's community began to exercise a powerful influence on social structures. People have often been surprised that there are so few direct references in the epistles, or elsewhere in the New Testament, to public witness and proclamation. This is because the community itself was living proof that the grace of God had appeared, bringing salvation to all. . . . It was clear that society did not have to be ruled by force or by exploitation. The community proved otherwise. It represented an alternative, a new life-style. Love, togetherness, brotherhood still seemed possible (Conrad Boerma, *The Rich, the Poor—and the Bible,* p. 74).

Just one theologian's opinion? A century ago another writer observed: "If we would humble ourselves before God, and be kind and courteous and tenderhearted and pitiful, there would be one hundred conversions where now there is only one" (Ellen White, *Welfare Ministry,* p. 86). One hundred to one—a hyperbole perhaps, but the point is inescapable, isn't it? Jesus is clear: The most potent and powerful force to convert our postmodern world will be our primitive kindness and love to one another—just like the church in the beginning.

"See how these Christians love each other."

"See how these Adventists love one another."

"A specially tender love for all of the same faith."

---

[1] www.cbsnews.com/stories/2002/11/14/national/main529380.shtml

[2] Zdravko Plantak's article, "Why should the Poor Concern Us?" in the *Adventist Review* (November 2002) has been helpful for me in examining egalitarianism in the context of the Bible witness.

[3] For a third millennial application of Jesus' execution-eve command to His followers, see my book *The Eleventh Commandment* (Pacific Press® Publishing Association, 2001).

CHAPTER FIVE

THE SHABBAT SHALOM OF THE POOR

On a Monday evening in Kansas City, Missouri, Joe R. Thompson III, eighteen years old, was driving down the highway in his Jeep, when through no fault of his own, another car suddenly turned in front of him. Joe swerved to miss the car, but clipped it on the back, after which his Jeep rolled over, eyewitnesses say, possibly up to five times. During one of those rolls, the fiberglass roof of the Jeep was ripped off, and Joe, who was *not* wearing his seat belt, was catapulted twenty-five feet into the air. In that awful trajectory, he hit something and instinctively grabbed hold of it. It was a utility power line, which fortunately for Joe was insulated and from which he hung for twenty long minutes as a rescue crew scrambled to bring him down. His father rushed to the scene. "I was told he was hanging on for dear life," Joe Thompson II said. "I didn't know they meant he literally was hanging on for dear life!"[1]

Joe was saved, but not everyone who's hanging on for dear life is as fortunate.

The headline in our local paper caught my eye: "Homeless falling through the cracks." And I don't suppose the news release for our community is much different from the community where you live (except perhaps for our chilling winters):

An icy wind pierced the thin jackets and bare hands of people huddled against the cold, heading for the Benton Harbor Soup Kitchen on a recent winter day. Once inside, the men, women, and children—black and white, old and young—were able to address at least one common problem: hunger. A host of other basic needs— shelter, heat, electricity, running water, a hot shower—went unmet that day, and for many days afterward for these and other of Berrien County's homeless and "precariously housed" residents.

"Young single-parent families with children are the fastest-growing component of the area's homeless population," said Jim Kehrer, chairman of the volunteer Homeless Resolution Network. "It's a group of people that doesn't fit neatly into any category for targeted services, so they aren't easily identified and they often just slip through the cracks."

"Any blip in your employment situation, even just one week without a paycheck, is a catastrophe when you're living hand-to-mouth, using everything you're making just to survive," Kehrer said. . . . "Being homeless means you've lost the most fundamental physical needs. . . . *You're hanging by a thread every day of your life.*"[2]

Hanging by a thread for dear life. But the poor aren't always as fortunate as Joe R. Thompson III, are they? All too often no rescuer ever shows up.

But in order that that would not happen, God pleads with His people in Isaiah 58: " 'Is not this the kind of fasting I have chosen: to loose the chains of injustice and untie the cords of the yoke, to set the oppressed free and break every yoke?' " (Isaiah 58:6).

It is a compelling call for social justice. Last year we convened a new task force—Solidarity with the Poor—here in the Pioneer Memorial Church. It is composed of university faculty, community social workers, area business people, and some students. The mission of this task force is to help us prioritize the needs of our community and the nearby inner city and assist us in developing a strategy to keep Isaiah 58's call before us as a campus and congregation.

I listened to these community activists describe how we need to take very seriously God's call to social justice in Isaiah 58:6. The inner-city poor are enchained by cycles of ignorance and misfortune. Unless they can be given skills and tools, they will remain in economic and social bondage. And it is a bondage, an oppression not unlike a war.

A few months ago, I was going door-to-door on a Sabbath afternoon in Benton Harbor (the inner city twelve miles from our campus) with our university students. The students have taught me a very simple strategy to get to know the residents of that city: "Hi, I'm Dwight, and this is Brad. We're from Andrews University, and we wanted to come by and pray with you. Do you have any special prayer needs?" I've been amazed at how that simple testimony on a doorstep can open up conversation and a unique opportunity to pray with a stranger.

So Brad and I went door-to-door, praying with people. At the end of one block we came to what looked like some sort of business establishment. It had a Cadillac parked in front with a bumper sticker proclaiming, "Jesus is Lord." *This ought to be a friendly establishment!* I thought. So we stomped the snow off our shoes and tromped through the front door to discover it was a beauty salon. I called out, "Who owns that car out front with the sticker 'Jesus is Lord' on it?" The place went dead silent. I hurried on, "Because, we're from Andrews University, and we're out praying with people, and we knew there would be friends in here!" With that everyone started talking and smiling as we fell into conversation. And when we were through, the whole salon bowed their heads as we prayed together.

Before that prayer, one of the male customers made a comment to me I will not forget. We somehow got to talking about the war in Iraq, and this man told me he had fought in Vietnam. "In fact," he went on, "I live in Vietnam."

"You live now in Vietnam?"

He nodded. And then with a hand pointing out the door, he clarified, "I live in Vietnam here in Benton Harbor." And then I realized his point. And I was surprised with his candor. Even the occupants of the city consider it a war zone.

Last summer that same inner city erupted in three days of rioting. The newspaper headlines read, "It's a war zone." But then, the impoverished heart of every city is precisely that, isn't it? The war zones of social injustice and substance abuse and economic and spiritual poverty are no respecters of cities or communities or countries.

God is sending His people into those war zones through Isaiah's passionate appeal:

> "Is not this the kind of fasting I have chosen:
> to loose the chains of injustice
>   and untie the cords of the yoke,
> to set the oppressed free
>   and break every yoke?
> Is it not to share your food with the hungry
>   and to provide the poor wanderer with shelter—
> when you see the naked, to clothe him,
>   and not to turn away from your own flesh and
> blood?" (Isaiah 58:6, 7).

The divine summons here to take up the cause for social justice and social action on behalf of disenfranchised, alienated, helpless human beings is clarion. No matter what nation or city or village we live in, existing economic systems or social infrastructures that enchain or entrap the poor must be challenged and changed. God cries out, "I am calling you to 'loose the chains of injustice' and to 'set the oppressed free.' "

John R. W. Stott, one of the twentieth century's most influential evangelical pastor-evangelists, is right:

> The cross is a revelation of God's justice as well as of his love. That is why the community of the cross should concern itself with social justice as well as loving philanthropy. It is never enough to have pity on the victims of injustice, if we do nothing to change the unjust situation itself. Good Samaritans will

always be needed to succor those who are assaulted and robbed; yet it would be even better to rid the Jerusalem-Jericho road of brigands. Just so Christian philanthropy in terms of relief and aid is necessary, but long term development is better, and we cannot evade our political responsibility to share in changing the structures which inhibit development. Christians cannot regard with equanimity the injustices which spoil God's world and demean his creatures. Injustice must bring pain to the God whose justice flared brightly at the cross; it should bring pain to God's people too (John R. W. Stott, *The Cross of Christ,* pp. 292, 293).

It is not enough to assist the needy. God calls His people to break the social and economic bonds that shackled the poor in the first place. And there are the chains of ignorance as well as injustice. Our task force, Solidarity with the Poor, has pointed us to the crying needs of cities everywhere for individuals who can teach and train residents in such basic skills as health improvement, finance management, child training, etc. We don't need to invent new social agencies. Often there are more than enough existing agencies through which we can volunteer our services as we join forces to break the cycles of despair.

Living as I do in a university community, I am often reminded how rich our congregations are in nonmonetary resources. An anonymous postcard sent to me the other day only confirms that realization. I've gotten my share of anonymous mail. And normally I don't read mail that isn't signed, since if the writer didn't feel it worth enough to sign it, how could it possibly be worth enough to read? But this little postcard was certainly the exception to that rule. For on it were handwritten these words:

Whatever you may possess above your fellows places you in debt, to that degree, to all who are less favored. Have we wealth, or even the comforts of life, then we are under the most solemn obligation to care for the suffering sick, the widow, and the fatherless exactly as we would desire them to care for us were our condition and theirs to be reversed. . . .

When those who profess the name of Christ shall practice the principles of the golden rule, the same power will attend the gospel as in apostolic times (Ellen White, *Thoughts From the Mount of Blessing,* pp.136, 137).

What a powerful reminder! It's why I'm grateful for community service action programs, such as the one on our campus or similar programs on other campuses, that train students how to become compassionate trainers themselves, volunteer helpers for the poor who need the knowledge we have. "Whatever you may possess above your fellows places you in debt, to that degree, to all who are less favored." What a solemn thought. It's the old principle of "to whom much is given, much is required" (see Luke 12:48).

Are you surprised that in Isaiah 58 God injects social justice and social action into the job description of His chosen people? Not only does He do so, but He makes social justice and social action the centerpieces between the bookends!

I happen to belong to a community of faith that loves to champion God's great Ss. First, there's salvation. Then there are the two Ss of the two bookends in Isaiah 58—the Sabbath and the sanctuary. And then comes the Second Advent. Then the state of the dead. And I suppose the Ss could go on and on. But Isaiah 58 is clear: Without social action and social justice, all the other Ss in the world won't fulfill God's mission.

Jesus once performed a miracle on the Sabbath that powerfully corroborates that point.

Then he went over to the synagogue, where he noticed a man with a deformed hand. The Pharisees asked Jesus, "Is it legal to work by healing on the Sabbath day?"(They were, of course, hoping he would say yes, so they could bring charges against him.)

And he answered, "If you had one sheep, and it fell into a well on the Sabbath, wouldn't you get to work and pull it out? Of course you would. And how much more valuable is a person than a sheep! Yes, it is right to do good on the Sabbath." Then he said to the man, "Reach out your hand." The man reached out his hand, and it became normal, just like the other one. Then the Pharisees called a meeting and discussed plans for killing Jesus (Matthew 12:9-14, NLT).

Do you know why they were so ticked? The Pharisees were furious because Jesus had just declared that their passionate defense of the right *day* was bankrupt without a passionate display of the right *way*. All that proper orthodoxy was bankrupted by their neglected orthopraxy. They had the *day* of the Sabbath right. But they were dead wrong about the *way* of the Sabbath.

And what is the right way? "It is right to do good on the Sabbath" (Matthew 12:12, NLT). For that reason Jesus reserved seven of His greatest healings for the seventh day of the week. Seven times on the seventh day Jesus chose to lead us straight into the broken heart of human need. "It is right to do good on the Sabbath." He who told us so is the One who said "I am the way and the truth and the life" (John 14:6). How then can we go wrong with social action and the Sabbath if we follow the way of Jesus?

No wonder God links his passionate appeal for social action and justice with an appeal for the Sabbath. Because, remember, orthodoxy (the right day) is meaningless without orthopraxy (the right way). That's why Isaiah 58 ends the way it does!

> "If you keep your feet from breaking the Sabbath
> and from doing as you please on my holy day,
> if you call the Sabbath a delight
> and the LORD's holy day honorable,
> and if you honor it by not going your own way
> and not doing as you please or speaking idle words,

then you will find your joy in the LORD,
> and I will cause you to ride on the heights of the land
and to feast on the inheritance of your father Jacob"
> > The mouth of the LORD has spoken (Isaiah 58:13, 14).

Isn't that something! God starts out talking about social justice and social action. And He ends up with a soliloquy on Sabbath observance. As if to say, "You'll get My day right, only when you get My way right." A point made a century ago as well:

> According to the fourth commandment the Sabbath was dedicated to rest and religious worship. All secular employment was to be suspended, but works of mercy and benevolence were in accordance with the purpose of the Lord. . . . *To relieve the afflicted, to comfort the sorrowing, is a labor of love that does honor to God's holy day* (Ellen White, *Welfare Ministry,* p. 77, emphasis supplied).

There it is—the perfect solution for a time-impoverished postmodern community of faith. Do we have little money and no time left for the poor? Jesus declares, "It is right to do good on the Sabbath." Which being interpreted means, *Sabbath afternoons are a gift from God through you to the poor, the suffering, the lonely, and the needy!* Do you need to be with your family? Then take your family with you to be with the needy . . . on a Sabbath afternoon. Do you want to be with your friends? Then take your friends with you to the poor . . . on a Sabbath afternoon. Do you want to enjoy the Sabbath rest? Then take the rest of Jesus to someone in need . . . on a Sabbath afternoon.

And if you'd like an even more specific list, take a look at one of these:
- Outreach to inner-city poor.
- "Sunshine Bands"—hospitals or foster care homes.
- Nursing home visitation (singing, reading, praying groups).
- Invite a poor family home for Sabbath dinner.

- Adopt a student for *any* dinner!
- Start a "Sabbath Meal on Wheels" ministry for shut-ins.
- Write letters and cards to the lonely (ask your pastor for names).
- Create and maintain a personal Web site for the lonely.
- Help your neighbor with his "sheep" in the well (emergency care).
- Shovel a senior citizen's driveway (find creative alternative in Florida!).
- _____ (Fill in your own ministry).

Sabbath afternoons are a gift from God through you to the poor, the suffering, the lonely, and the needy. For us time-impoverished postmoderns who really truly desire to embrace Jesus' solidarity with the poor, *isn't the Sabbath the perfect gift?* No wonder Jesus said, " 'The Sabbath was made to benefit people, and not people to benefit the Sabbath' " (Mark 2:27, NLT).

And can you think of a people more in need of His benefits than the poor? Unless, of course, you're thinking of you and me, which He was, when He gave us *the rest* of our lives in the Sabbath. "Come to Me . . . and I will give you rest" (Matthew 11:28, NKJV).

Shabbat shalom, indeed.

"Sabbath peace be with you."

"And with you, too."

<hr>

[1]Associated Press, January 29, 2003, www.joeha.com/wbnjan292003.htm.
[2] *Herald-Palladium,* February 16, 2003, emphasis supplied.

CHAPTER SIX

QUID PRO QUO

I met President Jimmy Carter a week ago. Well, I didn't actually shake his hand, but I sat six rows from him when the former president came to Benton Harbor, Michigan, to launch his "2005 Jimmy Carter Work Project" with Habitat for Humanity. In 2005, he and volunteers from across our community as well as our nation will descend on that inner city and build homes for some very fortunate residents. So last week the auditorium was packed to welcome the first former president to ever visit Benton Harbor.

I listened carefully to what this Nobel Peace Prize laureate had to say. And I must admit that, regardless of your political persuasion, you can't help but admire this humble Christian gentleman, once the most powerful man on earth, who now devotes his life to global peace and the eradication of poverty—and who still teaches Sunday School every weekend he's home in Plains, Georgia. I took notes as the former president addressed the crowd.

He told us that he and his wife, Rosalyn, had just returned from a visit to three African nations, and he observed that the problems there are not unlike the challenges our own nation and Benton Harbor face. He then stated, "The greatest problem the world faces today is the growing divide between the rich and the poor." He went on to point out that 1.2 billion people live on a dollar a day or less and that one-half the world's population lives on two dollars a day or less!

Clearly the former president is passionate about the need to eradicate poverty in all our communities, in all the countries of earth. And he issued a rousing call for everyone present to join him and Habitat for Humanity next year in seeking to reverse the poverty in Benton Harbor and revive the life of that inner city. Then to a standing ovation, President Carter with his trademark grin waved Goodbye until he returns next year.

But you don't have to be a former president to have the poor on your heart, do you? As Isaiah 58 keeps reminding us, even God has the poor very much on His mind and heart. And Isaiah 58 is clear that that is precisely where He wants us to have them, too.

This is so much so that God is prepared to make us an offer we cannot resist. Not one of those infamous inner-city mobster kind of offers—but, instead, one of the most persuasive *quid pro quo* offers you'll find anywhere in the Holy Bible. In fact, what you are about to read is arguably God's second greatest *quid pro quo* offer ever made.

Quid pro quo is Latin, meaning, "this for that," and it is usually couched in language such as, *"If* you'll do this, *then* I'll do that." Parents are *quid pro quo* specialists! "Junior, *if* you help me with the lawn today, *then* I'll take you to Great America next Sunday." That works great when your children are young, but as every dad knows, the value of your offer needs to ascend in direct proportion to your kids' age—until you're promising them your entire inheritance just to get that strip of lawn mowed!

The offer God makes in Isaiah 58 would have to be His *second* greatest *quid pro quo* offer, since clearly the greatest offer of all is His offer of eternal life: ". . . that whoever believes in Him *[quid]* should not perish but have everlasting life *[quo]*" (see John 3:16). So what would be His second greatest offer? I believe it's what God promises to all those who will embrace His own solidarity with the poor. *"If* you'll take care of My poor children *[quid], then* I'll . . . *[quo].* "And in the heart of

Isaiah 58 is the phenomenal *quo* that God is promising. What is more, you're about to read research evidence that empirically proves that God's *quo* is indeed worth writing home about.

Let's turn now to Isaiah 58 and notice its unmistakable *quid pro quo* language and offer.

> "Is not this the kind of fasting I have chosen:
> to loose the chains of injustice
>   and untie the cords of the yoke,
> to set the oppressed free
>   and break every yoke?
> Is it not to share your food with the hungry
>   and to provide the poor wanderer with shelter—
> when you see the naked, to clothe him,
>   and not to turn away from your own flesh and
> blood?" (Isaiah 58:6, 7).

"But wait a minute," you protest, "there's no *quid pro quo* language here." And of course, you're right. But the moment we read the very next line, it becomes clear we are in *quid pro quo* country.

> "Then your light will break forth like the dawn,
>   and your healing will quickly appear;
> then your righteousness will go before you,
>   and the glory of the LORD will be your rear guard"
> (verse 8).

Notice the *"then."* That means that what precedes it is an *"if."* And that makes this the *if-then* proposition of a *quid pro quo*.

In fact, when we insert the implied *ifs* and highlight the rest of the intentional *ifs* and *thens,* Isaiah 58 becomes a very compelling *quid pro quo* proposition from God to you and me! To help us visually see it, let's put in all caps the *ifs* and *thens* that are already in this passage, bracketing the *if you wills* and *thens* that are clearly implied in the passage. The verse numbers are included, so that you can compare this passage in your own Bible. Here we go:

6 "Is not this the kind of fasting I have chosen:
[IF YOU WILL] loose the chains of injustice
     and untie the cords of the yoke,
[IF YOU WILL] set the oppressed free
     and break every yoke?
7 [IF YOU WILL] share your food with the hungry
     and [IF YOU WILL] provide the poor wanderer
with shelter—
when you see the naked, [IF YOU WILL] clothe him,
     and [IF YOU WILL] not turn away from your own
flesh and blood?
8 THEN your light will break forth like the dawn,
     and your healing will quickly appear;
THEN your righteousness will go before you,
     and the glory of the LORD will be your rear guard.
9 THEN you will call, and the LORD will answer;
     you will cry for help, and he will say: Here am I"
(Isaiah 58:6-9, emphasis supplied).

"*If* you will embrace my solidarity with the poor," God cries out, "*then* I am going to supernaturally bless you in ways you never have experienced before!" But please note that He isn't through yet! In fact God repeats Himself just to make sure we understand that this is indeed a divine *quid pro quo!*

"IF you do away with the yoke of oppression,
     with the pointing finger and malicious talk,
10 and IF you spend yourselves in behalf of the hungry
     and satisfy the needs of the oppressed,
THEN your light will rise in the darkness,
     and your night will become like the noonday.
11 [THEN] the LORD will guide you always;
     he will satisfy your needs in a sun-scorched land
     and will strengthen your frame.

[THEN] you will be like a well-watered garden,
    like a spring whose waters never fail.
12 [THEN] your people will rebuild the ancient ruins
    and will raise up the age-old foundations;
you will be called Repairer of Broken Walls,
    Restorer of Streets with Dwellings.
13 "IF you keep your feet from breaking the Sabbath
    and from doing as you please on my holy day,
IF you call the Sabbath a delight
    and the LORD's holy day honorable,
and IF you honor it by not going your own way
    and not doing as you please or speaking idle words,
14 THEN you will find your joy in the LORD,
    and I will cause you to ride on the heights of the land
    and to feast on the inheritance of your father Jacob."
    The mouth of the LORD has spoken (Isaiah 58:9-14,
emphasis supplied).

Before we examine the empirical evidence that in fact God really does provide these phenomenal benefits and supernatural blessings, let's be sure we understand what we have just read by itemizing what is included in this dynamite *quid pro quo*:

If you will:

- Loose the chains of injustice.
- Set the oppressed free.
- Share your food with the hungry.
- Provide the homeless with shelter.
- Clothe the naked.
- Care for your own flesh and blood.
- Quit your accusing and malicious talk.
- Spend the Sabbath in My way.

Then I will:

- Shine My light upon you.
- Heal you.

- Go before you and behind you to protect you.
- Answer when you call upon Me.
- Guide you always.
- Satisfy your needs.
- Strengthen your bones.
- Water your garden.
- Raise up a new generation to rebuild your foundation.
- Honor you throughout the land.

Larry Ulrey, director of the Andrews University Community Service Action Program, calls this "God's algorithm for limitless blessing." And he's right! For essentially God is saying, "I hereby promise you that if you will embrace My solidarity with the poor, I will bless you and bless you and bless you—spiritually, intellectually, emotionally, physically, and financially."

But you say, "I don't see anything here about God blessing me *financially* if I embrace His solidarity with the poor!"

You're right; it isn't explicitly stated here in Isaiah 58. But it is implied as seen by these four supporting verses:

- "If you help the poor, you are lending to the LORD—and he will repay you!" (Proverbs 19:17, NLT).
- " 'If you give, you will receive. Your gift will return to you in full measure, pressed down, shaken together to make room for more, and running over. Whatever measure you use in giving—large or small—it will be used to measure what is given back to you' " (Luke 6:38, NLT).
- " ' "It is more blessed to give than to receive" ' " (Acts 20:35).
- "The generous prosper and are satisfied; those who refresh others will themselves be refreshed" (Proverbs 11:25, NLT).

There they are—four more *quid pro quo* promises that encompass even the financial dimension of our daily lives! God says, "Embrace the poor on My behalf—give to them as you would give to Me—and I will bless you and bless you and bless you and bless you."

But can You prove it, God?

Can He prove it! Let's take a look at some startling empirical evidence that all of this "algorithm for limitless blessing" is, in fact, true! My friend and colleague Skip MacCarty, one of our pastors here at Pioneer Memorial Church, has written a nationally recognized book on stress, *Stress: Beyond Coping*. Let me share with you some studies from his research that empirically corroborate what God has just promised.

Study #1

There was a fascinating study done at Harvard University, where 132 students were shown "a powerful 50-minute film of Nobel Laureate Mother Teresa aiding the sick and dying of Calcutta." When the film was over, the students were tested for the amount of Immunoglobulin A (IgA for short) in their saliva. IgA is part of the body's defense against certain viruses. Those students who had seen the film had increases in this measure of their immune system function. The researchers called it the "Mother Teresa effect." And they also found that those *students who had the most positive results were those who expressed a desire to be involved in some effort to also help others,* even if they knew that the help they could give wouldn't completely solve the problems of the people they were trying to help or perhaps might not even be all that appreciated by them. Their rewards would be intrinsic rather than extrinsic. Those students showed the greatest increase in the IgA measure of their immune system function (Allan Luks with Peggy Payne, *The Healing Power of Doing Good* [New York: Fawcett Columbine, 1991], pp. 87, 180-184, emphasis supplied).

Isn't that amazing? Apparently, just watching somebody else minister to the poor can boost your immune system! Which, of course, is not an excuse for hanging around the Community Services center or driving through an inner city just so you can watch others serve the needy.

Because as the Harvard study noted, the students with the greatest immune system boost were the ones who wanted to get into the thick of the action of helping others, even if they knew there would be no monetary rewards or measurable success.

How did God put it? Become a helper to those in need, and "your healing will come quickly" (Isaiah 58:8, NLT). Harvard University says He's right.

Study #2

A major study of elderly people conducted by the Federal Retired Senior Volunteer Program (RSVP) found health improvements among volunteers that seemed miraculous. In 98 percent of these federal facilities studied, the physical and mental health of the RSVP members had improved significantly. Alfred Larson, the then National Director of RSVP, reported: "Doctors always tell us that elderly people who engage in volunteer work are a lot better off, visit the doctor less often, and have fewer complaints" (Luks, *Healing Power*, p. 233).

So now we know that it isn't only the young who benefit from public service. The elderly reap health benefits, too. How did God put it? " 'Then your light will shine out from the darkness, and the darkness around you will be as bright as day' " (Isaiah 58:10, NLT). The elderly know all about a sense of darkness. But God promises shining light in the midst of their dimming years. No wonder our community services volunteers live so well, and many of them live so long!

Study #3

Here's another study Skip reports on in his book on stress:

A ten-year study of the physical health and social activities of 2,700 men of all ages in Tecumseh, Michigan, found that those who did regular volunteer work had death rates two and one half times lower than those who didn't" (Douglas M. Lawson, Ph.D., *Give to Live* [La Jolla, Calif.: ALTI Publishing, 1991], p. 20).

Now there's an appealing masculine *quid pro quo*. *If* you men will invest your lives in public service and community volunteering, *then* your death rate will be two and a half times lower than that of your too-busy-to-volunteer-for-anything buddies. How about that offer! God's promise is, " 'The LORD will guide you always; he will satisfy your needs in a sun-scorched land and will strengthen your frame' " (Isaiah 58:11).

Study #4

In 1987 Kristine Orth-Gomer reported on a research project conducted by the Swedish National Institute for Psychological Factors and Health in which 17,000 people randomly selected from the entire population of Sweden were studied for six years. One of the significant findings of that research was that the socially isolated people in that study died at a rate almost four times higher than did people who were socially involved (Luks, *Healing Power,* p. 32).

Our immersion in community, our hanging around other people, our physical and emotional and social contacts with other human beings—we were created for that kind of fellowship, weren't we? Tracking 17,000 people for six years revealed that without that human interaction we face a death rate four times higher than the Isaiah 58 types who make people their passion. " 'If you spend yourselves in behalf of the hungry and satisfy the needs of the oppressed,' " (Isaiah 58:10)—that is, if you'll keep yourself immersed in the matrix of human need and human association, look at how God promises to bless your life!

Allan Luks coined a phrase to describe this multifaceted boost that we experience when we become involved in the lives of others. Skip notes that his phrase now is part of the vernacular of researchers in this field of study. It's called "the helper's high." Luks summarizes the studies: "The results of these . . . health benefits to the helper (volunteer) . . . can be astonishing in their impact. Helping contributes to the maintenance of good health, and it can diminish the effect of diseases and disorders both serious and minor, psychological and physical" (Luks, *Healing Power,* p. 83).

Science is corroborating what God has promised for thousands of years in Isaiah 58.

Study #5

Let me share one more study, this one from Larry Ulery's files:

> According to researchers at the Institute for the Advancement of Health, *doing regular volunteer work increases life expectancy.* The research suggests that the feeling of "warmth" that results from helping others can be attributed to the release of endorphins in the brain. Since nerve cells involved are connected to parts of the body that fight infection, *doing good can help your immune system.* Another study, conducted at the University of California Medical School in San Francisco, found that *volunteering "seems to increase self esteem, foster a sense of competence, and fight off stress and depression"* (MLI-LIT/LINE [Michigan Literacy Inc.]).

How many studies would it take for you and me to give serious consideration to God's incredible offer to supernaturally "boost" our lives on every front, if we would only embrace His unrelenting solidarity with the poor, with every human being in need?

" 'You will be like a well-watered garden, / like a spring whose waters never fail' " (Isaiah 58:11). God can't get more effusive than that, can He?

So shall we do it, with a panhandler's palm outstretched for His blessing? "OK, God, let's make a deal—*quid pro quo.* I do this, You do that; fair enough?" Something rings crassly hollow with such a proposition, doesn't it?

"If I give all I possess to the poor . . . but have not love, I gain nothing" (1 Corinthians 13:3). Paul is right. Life ultimately is not about a *quid pro quo* bargain with God or with the poor or with anyone else for that matter. Genuine life and authentic living flow from the wellsprings of self-sacrificing love, the *agape* love that Paul champions in his "Ode to Love" (see 1 Corinthians 13). Without it, all the philanthropy in the world is useless and pointless. As John Stott observes: "So love gives food to the hungry, shelter to the homeless, help to the destitute, friendship to the lonely, comfort to the sad, *provided always that these gifts are tokens of the giving of the self.* For it is possible to give food, money, time and energy, and yet somehow withhold oneself" (John R. W. Stott, *The Cross of Christ*, p. 292, emphasis supplied).

Without the giving of myself, without self-giving love as the deeper motivation, all my volunteering and serving and ministering amounts to little more than public genuflecting. "I gain nothing." (And as the Harvard University study noted, I won't even gain as much immune system boost from the "Mother Teresa effect.")

So where can we find the heart for such self-giving love? From the greatest *quid pro quo* story of all: "For God so loved the world that he gave his only Son" (John 3:16). Call it the "Jesus Christ effect." "For Christ's love compels us" (2 Corinthians 5:14, NIV).

I think of Domenico Feti's great painting, *Ecce Homo* ("Behold the Man"). It's a painting of Christ, the crown of thorns upon His bloody brow. And underneath, the artist inscribed upon a plaque these words, "All this I did for thee; what doest thou for Me?"

For Calvary reverses the *quid pro quo*, does it not? "All this I did for thee; what doest thou for Me?" *Quid pro quo*. Only now, we are no longer driven by what we can *get* from Him. In the shadows of that center cross, we are compelled to *give* back to Him. *Quid pro quo*.

And what shall we give, we who have already been given eternity in Him?

I attended a concert celebrating the thirtieth anniversary of REACH International, a humanitarian organization devoted to the loving care of orphans in the developing world.[1] On the cover of the anniversary brochure was this simple reading that perhaps answers that question, "What shall we give to Him?"

> On the street I saw a small girl,
> cold, shivering in a thin dress,
> with little hope of a decent meal.
> I became angry and said to God:
> "Why did you permit this?
> Why don't you do something about it?"
> For a while God said nothing.
> Then that night He replied quite suddenly:
> "I certainly did something about it.
> I made you."
>
> —Author Unknown

---

[1]For a year and a half now, our family has sponsored orphans through REACH International, P.O. Box 34, Berrien Springs, MI 49103. For $18 a month per child on a credit card, it's a simple but systematic way you can make a difference halfway around the world.

CHAPTER SEVEN

THE TRUTH OF THE TALKING BULL
(AN UNAPOLOGETIC APOLOGETIC)

I realize that what you're about to read might come across as audacious or presumptuous. But I am deeply burdened to write it. If you are young and you are still reading this book (that's the presumptuous part!), I believe you are reading right now because God has a message for you. And He has asked me to deliver the message to you (that's the audacious part).

Let me cut to the chase. God is calling you. And it falls my lot right now to relay that call to you. Here it is: If you are young—I don't care what your pursuit in life happens to be, academically or professionally, or what career you may have already settled into—*you are being called by God today to become a defender of the faith.* That's right, a third millennial defender of a very ancient faith.

Look, if a bull can talk (and I am going to end with an almost unbelievable, but true, story of a bull doing just that)—if a bull can talk, so can you.

I'm certain that those of us who are not as young as are the youth of today are also included in this message from God. But I am particularly burdened for you who are young—up into your thirties. So with all the earnestness I can muster, I need to say, "Please listen up!" Near the end of the Bible appears this solitary sentence: "Beloved, while I was making every effort to write you about our common salvation, I felt the necessity to write to you appealing that you contend earnestly for the faith which was once for all delivered to the saints" (Jude 3, NASB). So wrote Jude, the step-brother of Jesus. He candidly admitted that while he had been "very eager to write . . . about the salvation we share" (as the *New International Version* translates this line), for some reason his heart had become agitated and stirred up over an interrupting matter. And so pivoting on that digression, Jude switched to an urgent plea: "Contend earnestly for the faith which was once for all delivered to the saints."

In Greek, "contend earnestly" is but a single word: *agonizomai*—"to strive" or "to fight." Look at it long enough, and you will recognize the familiar English word *agonize*. When I agonize over something, I experience a deep inner striving or debating or even emotional or mental fighting. The Greek root *agon* was a stadium where those ancient fighting contests were held.

And what is it that Jude is appealing to us to agonize and fight and contend for? "For the faith which was once for all delivered to the saints." He doesn't refer here to personal faith or trust or belief. Clearly, Jude is summoning us to contend for "*the* faith," the great corpus or body of truth. His passion cuts to the point: *Become a mighty defender of the faith!*

I don't know which side of the Iraqi conflict you find yourself praying for these days. I hope you're praying for both and for a speedy cessation of violence and warfare. But it is clear that both sides believe they are the defenders. One side fervently believes it is *defending* freedom and liberty for all. The other side desperately believes it is *defending* homeland and security for all. But that's just the point: When you truly defend something, you are willing to fight and die for that something—if you truly believe in that something.

"Beloved, while I was making every effort to write you about our common salvation, I felt the necessity to write to you appealing that you contend earnestly for the faith which was once for all delivered to the saints" (Jude 3, NASB).

I like the way Eugene Peterson translates that line: " . . . fight with everything you have in you for this faith entrusted to us as a gift to

PURSUING THE
PASSION
OF JESUS

FOOD SECURITY

If you have food security, you're able to eat today, and you know where your next meal is coming from. ADRA's food security programs not only provide emergency food aid where necessary, but also teach families to take care of their own needs by providing the essential tools they need to grow their own crops and sell them at market. Hunger is the most extreme form of poverty, in which individuals or families cannot afford to meet their most basic need for food. At least 842 million people around the world are hungry today. *Hunger Report 2004, Bread for the World Institute.*

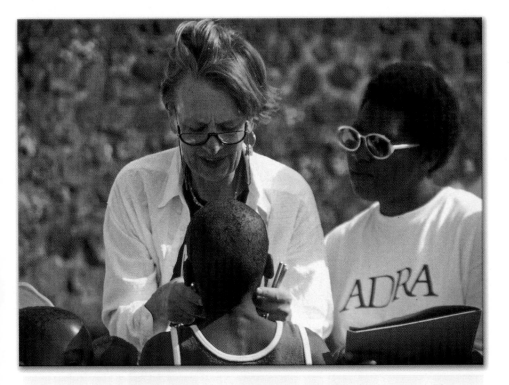

PRIMARY HEALTH CARE

Stifling the potential of children and parents in developing countries are the massive global HIV/AIDS epidemic, high birth and illiteracy rates, and a severe lack of access to adequate health care and potable water. Every year, more than ten million children die from preventable causes. The world knows what it takes to improve child health and survival, but millions continue to die because they lack access to these basic services. *United Nations Children's Fund (UNICEF).*

BASIC EDUCATION

For a nation to emerge from "developing country" status, it must educate its citizens. But education is a mere dream for millions of children worldwide. And even when limited education is available, girls are often denied access. They grow up to become uneducated mothers who are unable to take good care of their children, and the generations that follow remain stuck in a desperate, disempowered cycle. Of the 680 million children in developing countries, 115 million do not attend school. Three-fifths of these are girls. *Human Development Report 2003.*

ECONOMIC DEVELOPMENT

In countries lacking a reliable banking system or formal savings and credit institutions, or where services are denied to women and to those who live in poverty, ADRA steps in with an empowering hand. By partnering with groups, mostly women, and by establishing programs that are stepping stones to self-reliance, ADRA gives a hand up—not a handout. In the developing world, more than 1.2 billion people currently live below the international poverty line, earning less that $1 per day. *Human Development Report 2003*

DISASTER PREPAREDNESS AND RESPONSE

Responding quickly. Responding appropriately. Wars, famines, hurricanes, droughts, earthquakes, and flooding take devastating tolls on human life and inhibit development. With an effective, timely response, those affected by disasters will not only survive, but also thrive. At the start of 2004, the number of asylum seekers, refugees, internally displaced persons, returned refugees, and stateless persons in the world numbered 17 million. *United Nations High Commissioner for Refugees (UNHCR).*

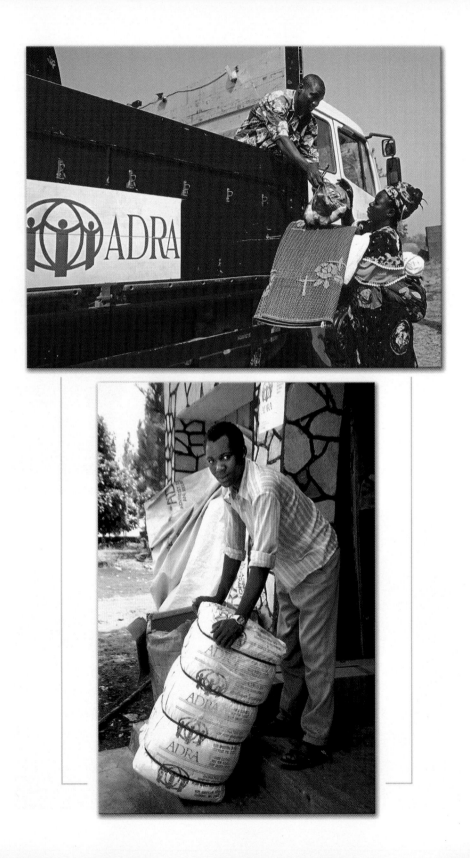

guard and cherish" (*The Message*). This is hardly house-to-house, hand-to-hand conflict. Jude is pleading for a mind-to-mind, intellect-to-intellect, heart-to-heart, person-to-person defense of the faith, the very corpus of the everlasting gospel.

But is it an outdated faith—this ancient faith "once for all" delivered to our forefathers and foremothers? Just ask God. "This is what the LORD says: 'Stand at the crossroads and look; ask for the ancient paths, ask where the good way is, and walk in it, and you will find rest for your souls.' " (Jeremiah 6:16). Or as the *New Living Translation* renders it: " 'Stop right where you are! Look for the old, godly way, and walk in it. Travel its path, and you will find rest for your souls.' "

We who are young (allow me that small vanity) must beware the notion that if it's old it's outdated. That's Madison Avenue's favorite line. "New and improved" is the advertisers' unsubtle mission to have us believe that our clothes are outmoded, our cars are outdated, and our hairstyles are outlandish. So the hypnotic chant incessantly blitzes our media—get rid of the old and bring in the new!

"Wrong!" God cries out. "My truth is like fine art—the older it gets the more valuable it becomes." "Do not remove the ancient landmark which your fathers have set" (Proverbs 22:28, NKJV). "Contend for the faith once for all delivered to the saints!"

And wouldn't you know it—in the very heart of Isaiah 58 *the very same passionate appeal is sounded.*

> "Your ancient ruins shall be rebuilt;
>> you shall raise up the foundations of many generations;
> you shall be called the repairer of the breach,
>> the restorer of streets to dwell in" (Isaiah 58:12, NRSV).

One of the glories of the countryside in England is its meandering matrix of ancient stone walls. They seem to be everywhere. From the towering stone edifices of Hadrian's first-century wall in northern England to the painstakingly crafted rock walls that wind and wend across the rolling hills of Yorkshire, they contain the mystery of an ancient beauty. Karen and I have walked and driven beside them for miles.

One of the realities of long-ago stone walls was that they were subject to breaching. Barbarian hordes, sweeping down from the north, sought to breach the wall of Roman emperor Hadrian by crashing against its ramparts, and eventually they succeeded. In contrast, the farmland walls of the shire were breached more subtly, broken down by the passage of time and the neglect of their builders—a collapsed stone here, a missing rock there—until a gaping breach was left.

Ancient Israel knew stone walls, too, and suffered the same breaches—whether by attack or through neglect—throughout their history. Seizing that metaphor, God passionately announces in the heart of Isaiah 58 that He will raise a *new* generation. "But," He declares, "I shall not ask them to do a new thing. Instead I will call this *new* generation to lead My people back to the *old*. To restore the *ancient* streets, to rebuild the *ancient* foundations, to repair the *ancient* walls. And they shall be called the 'Repairer of the Breach.' "

What breach could God be talking about? While there are numerous breaches one could suggest for possible application here, God doesn't leave us wondering. He offers a very huge clue in the two verses that follow:

> "If you keep your feet from breaking the Sabbath
> and from doing as you please on my holy day,
> if you call the Sabbath a delight
> and the LORD's holy day honorable,
> and if you honor it by not going your own way
> and not doing as you please or speaking idle words,
> then you will find your joy in the LORD,
> and I will cause you to ride on the heights of the land
> and to feast on the inheritance of your father Jacob."
> The mouth of the LORD has spoken
(Isaiah 58:13, 14).

On the night of May 16, 1943, a squadron of Royal Air Force bombers was dispatched on a strategic mission to destroy the Mohne Dam in the Ruhr Valley of Germany. Screaming up that midnight valley sixty feet off the ground, the bombers carried a specially designed piece of munitions called a "dam buster." Engineers calculated that the strategically dropped "dam buster" bomb could blast a single small hole in that massive concrete wall that would eventually cause it to explode as a consequence of the enormous water pressure behind the dam. And sure enough, the mission was a success. With billions of gallons of water attempting to flow through that small hole, the mighty dam could not withstand the pressure. Its wall was breached. And as a consequence, the dam blew open, washing 1,300 sleeping residents in the valley below to their death (see Glen Walker, *Prophecy Made Easy: Experience the Future Now!,* p. 153).

The juxtaposition of God's call for "Repairers of the Breach" with His appeal to honor His seventh-day Sabbath clearly identifies the breach God wants to be repaired. An enemy has targeted the towering, protective wall of God's law. But rather than blast its ten precepts to smithereens, the wily enemy knew that one strategically placed strike could bring the entire wall down. "For whoever keeps the whole law and yet stumbles at just one point is guilty of breaking all of it" (James 2:10). *The wall of God's law has been strategically breached at the fourth commandment in this third millennium.* The seventh-day Sabbath has been broken. God is calling for a new generation to repair that breach and restore that truth.

> "Your ancient ruins shall be rebuilt;
>   you shall raise up the foundations of many generations;
> you shall be called the repairer of the breach,
>   the restorer of streets to dwell in" (Isaiah 58:12, NRSV).

God needs a new generation to "contend earnestly for the faith once for all delivered to the saints" in the truth about the seventh-day Sabbath. Unfortunately the *old* generation has forgotten about the Sabbath. Huge tracts of Christendom now reject the Bible Sabbath in favor of Sunday worship, introduced over a millennium and a half ago by the church that would become the most influential institution of the Middle Ages (and that is rapidly regaining her previous ascendency).

But sadly enough huge numbers of people *within our own commu-nity of faith* have also abandoned—or at least forgotten—the sanctity and holiness of the Creator's gift of the seventh-day Sabbath. For them, Sabbath celebration has effectively been reduced to the hour or two (maybe three if they choose to attend Sabbath School) that they give to a formal gathering with others of like-minded faith on a Saturday morn-ing. Once "church" (as they call it) is over—then it's boating and biking and motoring and sleeping and eating and listening and watching and reading and socializing and packing and traveling and vacationing and dining out *just like any other day of their very ordinary and busy week*. For them, the seventh day is, effectively, only three hours long.

" 'If you keep your feet from breaking the Sabbath and from doing as you please on my holy day, if you call the Sabbath a delight and the LORD's holy day honorable, and if you honor it by not going your own way and not doing as you please or speaking idle words, then you will find your joy in the LORD, and I will cause you to ride on the heights of the land and to feast on the inheritance of your father Jacob.' The mouth of the LORD has spoken."

Ancient Jews believed that if they could all keep one Sabbath per-fectly, the Messiah would come. But that isn't what God is asking for here, is it? All He asks is to have quiet, uninterrupted communion with you and me for the twenty-four little hours of the seventh day of the week. His gift of the seventh-day Sabbath is for the celebration of a friendship with our forever Friend, our Creator—God the Father, God the Son, and God the Spirit.

That's why God longs for us to call the Sabbath "a delight." Not a day to sit at home in chains until sundown—of course not. But twenty-four hours in which to delight ourselves in Christ, so that *He* becomes the center of our Sabbath activity and our Sabbath rest. Sure, get to-gether with your friends—go and meet your neighbors—love and serve the poor—of course. But God appeals to us—do it *with* Me, do it *for* Me. "Remember Me!"

When I was a kid and went off from home for the first time to school—a boarding academy in Singapore—I used to love to hang around the upperclassmen guys. It made me feel important just being around them. But it used to really hurt when those older guys, as if on some prearranged cue, would suddenly walk off, not inviting me to join them. There I was, standing beside them—they saw me; they knew me. But they walked off as if I didn't even exist. And for a teenager's heart, what hurts more than feeling left out and unnoticed or worse yet, unwanted?

So how do you suppose God feels? He has given us this day to spend together with Him. How do you suppose He feels when on this day we just walk off and leave Him standing there? If an ignored teenage boy can hurt, can't an abandoned God hurt, too? "This was supposed to be *our* day together," He whispers sadly.

"Remember the Sabbath day to keep it holy" (Exodus 20:8). Is it that word *holy* that bothers us? Maybe we ought to start misspelling it. Maybe then we'd get it right. "Remember the Sabbath day to keep it *wholly.*" "Wholly for you and Me together," God invites us. It's the fourth commandment. In the heart of God's Decalogue. Written in stone with His own finger.

Of course "it is lawful to do good on the Sabbath," as we heard Jesus declare in a previous chapter. But I don't suppose God worries so much about our doing *good* on the Sabbath, as much as He must wonder if we do *God* on the Sabbath! "Do you do *Me* on My day?"

Let's face it, "God" and "good" and "goods" and "gods"—just the tweaking of a letter or two can make all the difference, can't it? A classified ad appeared in the newspaper: "GARAGE SALE. 19-inch color TV, golf clubs, refrigerator, and other household gods." One small typographical error, but it highlights the painful truth. We humans have that unique proclivity of being able to turn our goods into gods. And sad to say, we Sabbatarians have refined that proclivity—we've turned the Sabbath from God into just plain good.

"I know you can do *good* on My Sabbath, but do you ever do *God?* Do you ever do *Me?*"

Ronald J. Sider, in his provocative book *Rich Christians in an Age of Hunger,* notes how a genuine "practice of the Sabbath" releases us from the clutching grasp of materialism by drawing us more deeply into the presence of God:

> If Christians could recover the practice of the Sabbath, it would help us turn away from the mad consumerism that is destroying people and the environment. Almost everything in our culture undermines what the [F]ourth Commandment wisely insists on preserving. If the spirit of the Sabbath would truly penetrate our minds and values, we would long to rest our tired psyches, enjoy our families and neighbors, and take quiet delight in the presence of our God. . . . We would treasure this holy leisure more than the opportunity to use [Sabbath] to accomplish still one more important task, or build one more balcony in our Tower of Babel. And *in those quiet times in the divine presence,* the God of the poor would transform our materialistic hearts and make us more generous (*Rich Christians in an Age of Hunger: Moving from Affluence to Generosity,* p. 207, emphasis supplied).

In some inexplicable way, our Sabbath "quiet times in the divine presence" draw us not only closer to our God but closer to the objects of His own tender regard—the poor and the needy and the suffering.

No wonder the God of Isaiah 58 is so passionate about the Sabbath. Did you notice that He calls it, "My holy day" (Isaiah 58:13)? By the way, the blending of "holy" and "day" is the source of our modern word *holiday.* That makes the Sabbath our holiday with Him and His holiday with us! A holiday to "wholly" spend together.

I don't know an employee on earth that doesn't enjoy a holiday. Don't we all keep secretly hoping that Congress will find another worthy president or two or three (there surely must be some left) and declare a few more Mondays as holidays on our calendars? Guess what—we've got a Creator who has marked off a holiday for us at the end of every single week of the year! That computes to fifty-two holidays a year—every single seventh day. Who's complaining!

Maybe our problem is that we've misread Isaiah 58:14—" 'Then you will find your joy in the LORD.' " Perhaps for all these years we've read it, "Then you will find your joy in the *day.*" But that isn't how it reads. The Sabbath is an invitation to delight in the *Giver* more than in the *gift.*

When I fell in love with Karen in college, I showered her with gifts—flowers, trinkets (a euphemism for junk, I suppose), and little 45 records of our love song (in case you don't know, 45s were those little round black disks that you put on a machine called a phonograph; they spun in circles dragging a scratchy little needle through the record's grooves, thereby creating the sounds of music). Why all those gifts? Because I wanted Karen to know that I loved her—as only a nineteen-year-old boy can love. But I'd have been really hurt if she'd become more preoccupied with my gifts than she was with me, if she had gone off and forgotten all about me—the giver.

The Sabbath is a holiday that invites us to delight in the Giver more than the gift. But some of us have become so preoccupied trying to prove on which day of the week the gift is supposed to come that, for all practical purposes, we've blanked the Giver right out of the picture! We can prove the *day* from the Bible, but have we, like Israel, forgotten the *way?*

I believe that is the case to a far greater extent than we realize. And I believe that is why God is going to raise up a new generation within our community of faith—*a new generation that will "contend earnestly for the faith once for all delivered to the saints" regarding the truth about the seventh-day Sabbath.* For how can we possibly defend the gift of the seventh day to the world when we don't even remember the Giver of the seventh day ourselves?

"If you turn back your foot from the sabbath,
     from doing your pleasure on my holy day,
and call the sabbath a delight
     and the holy day of the LORD honorable;

if you honor it, not going your own ways,
> or seeking your own pleasure, or talking idly;
then you shall take delight in the LORD,
> and I will make you ride on the heights of the earth;
I will feed you with the heritage of Jacob your father,
> for the mouth of the LORD has spoken"
(Isaiah 58:13, 14, RSV).
"And your ancient ruins shall be rebuilt;
> you shall raise up the foundations
of many generations;
you shall be called the repairer of the breach,
> the restorer of streets to dwell in" (verse 12).

Less than a century ago these words were written:

> In the time of the end every divine institution is to be restored. The breach made in the law at the time the Sabbath was changed by man, is to be repaired. God's remnant people, *standing before the world as reformers*, are to show that the law of God is the foundation of all enduring reform and that the Sabbath of the fourth commandment is to stand as a memorial of creation, a constant reminder of the power of God. In clear, distinct lines they are to present the necessity of obedience to all the precepts of the Decalogue. *Constrained by the love of Christ, they are to co-operate with Him in building up the waste places. They are to be repairers of the breach, restorers of paths to dwell in* (Ellen White, *Prophets and Kings*, p. 678, emphasis supplied).

"Contend earnestly for the faith once for all delivered to the saints." "And you shall be called the Repairer of the Breach." I repeat, God is calling you to become a mighty defender of His faith!

But you say, "I can't do that! I'm too timid, too reserved, too sensitive to being politically correct, too shy." Oh, yes, you can be a defender, my friend. Do you know why? Because you're a follower of Jesus, and He's going to take care of you.

Get this: He has already promised that He will personally provide every one of His followers with the *courage* as well as the *content* for their defense of the faith: " 'Don't worry about what to say in your defense, for the Holy Spirit will teach you what needs to be said *even as you are standing there*" (Luke 12:11, 12, NLT, emphasis supplied). Be at peace. He'll not only give you the courage to speak up for Him, He's promised to also give you the content for that speaking up—on the spot!

"Go and defend My faith, for I am with you always!" God is calling you to become a mighty defender of the faith. No matter your academic discipline. No matter your career choice. You are first and foremost called to contend for the faith and repair the breach.

For if a bull can talk—so can you!

Here is a story so nearly unbelievable that I had to read it over again and again. I accept its veracity, for I know the one who related the story to me. David Tasker is a doctoral graduate (Ph.D.) of Andrews University. Now dean of the school of theology at Pacific Adventist University in Papua New Guinea, he and his wife Carol were New Zealander graduate students on our board of elders here at Pioneer Memorial Church before they took up their new post of service.

David learned of this story through his interview of an indigenous pastor, James Manele. David sent me the transcription of the taped interview, which I have condensed and edited.[1]

The story comes from the Kwaibaita ("big river") village, which is beside an inland river in the eastern part of Malaita, Solomon Islands, and concerns the paramount chief of that village. The village was a South Sea Evangelical Church village (apparently, predominantly Christian villages are identified by their dominant churches), and the paramount chief was also the pastor of the village, having served as pastor for the previous twenty years. "So he had quite a lot of respect from his people."

However, every time nurses and medical workers from the Atoifi Seventh-day Adventist hospital would come to this village to help the people, the chief (pastor) would warn the villagers: "You can accept their medications but not their teachings. If they tell you anything about the Bible or the church, just ignore it. Accept their medications but not their teachings." And the people would dutifully obey their pastor and chief.

But the paramount chief began to feel guilty for forbidding his villagers to listen to the Adventists, and his conscience began to bother him. Then it was that "sometime in September of that year . . . he experienced something that happened which drastically changed his life."

One Sabbath morning (a "Saturday morning" as far as the chief was concerned), he and his wife and child went to visit their garden a short distance from the village. To get there they needed to pass through a cow paddock that enclosed about ten cows along with some goats. When they walked through the paddock, "something strange happened." The cows all lined up and faced the approaching chief, "like soldiers on parade." But they didn't part, as the chief expected them to when he approached them. That meant the chief and his family had to walk around that straight line of cows in order to get past them. And at the end of the line was a bull, "big and fat." But as the chief approached the bull, it didn't move. "Instead it suddenly spoke in the Kwaibaita language. It said, 'Why did you come to the garden at this time? Don't you know that today is the seventh day, the Sabbath of the Lord God?' "

"The chief was shocked." (And who wouldn't be?) He "looked around to check if it was a mistake. The voice was coming from the bull, and as it was talking, the mouth was moving when it spoke." The chief (his name was Timothy) was finally able to ascertain that it really was the bull talking to him. The bull spoke again: " 'Timothy, I am speaking to you. Timothy!' " The chief "was brought to attention!" He stood there shaking, for he had never heard an animal talk before. His wife and child also heard the bull speaking.

The chief cried out, " 'There must be a devil in you, talking like that.' " And the bull responded by saying: " 'I am not the devil. I'm the voice of Jesus speaking to you.' Timothy [now] gave the bull his attention [and] opened his ears." The bull continued: " 'Today is the Sabbath of God. Don't you know that God gave you six days to work and the seventh is the Sabbath? Don't you know that? You have been a pastor, and yet you don't know these things? How blind can you be? God gave you six days to work; the seventh day is the Sabbath. You must not work today in your garden. Go home and read Jeremiah 1:5 [" 'Before I formed you in the womb I knew you; before you were born I sanctified you' " (NKJV)]. And after you have read it, share it with your people and look for the Seventh-day Adventist pastor, whose name is Pastor Bata. And when you find the Adventist pastor, talk to him and he will further explain things to you.' Then the bull stopped talking."

By now, the chief was "horrified" and fell to the ground sobbing. "He cried because this was a rebuke to him." Finally he stood again and told his wife " 'We must go back and rest. We must not work.' " So they returned to their village, and the chief called all the villagers together and told them the story of the talking bull. "So that day they did not do any work."

Early the next morning, Chief Timothy began a four-hour trek through mountain brush until he came to the Adventist hospital in Atoifi. There he introduced himself as the chief of Kwaibaita and said that he was looking for a Pastor Bata. " 'Who told you about Pastor Bata?' " What was the chief supposed to say now? That he was following the instructions of a bull? So he simply responded, " 'I have a story to tell to Pastor Bata.' " Whereupon the chief was taken to another village, where he met Pastor Bata and promptly told him the whole story. " 'I have already kept the Sabbath,' " the chief testified.

And so it was that Pastor Bata studied the Bible with Timothy for the next three months.

On the day of Chief Timothy's baptism, many people gathered to witness it. The pastor-chief "made a public confession and appealed for those who wanted to join him to stand on one side, and those who wished to remain as they were on the other side. The majority of the people joined him, so later they put up a little church and I [Pastor Jim Manele] was invited to dedicate the church."

Today there is a "very big church in a nearby village . . . funded and built by some Australians, and that church is now the centre of our work in that area."

That's the end of the story. That's the truth of the talking bull.

Now, you may be thinking, *I don't believe that story!* Which is precisely the point. God doesn't need a talking bull; He has *you* instead! But He does need *you* to start talking, because He needs someone where *you* live and where *you* study and where *you* work and where *you* play to "contend earnestly for the faith once for all delivered to the saints." Look, God can use a bull or an ass, if He has to. *But you are His first choice!*

Oh sure, Jesus declared that the stones will cry out if you and I don't. But God is raising up a *new* generation at the end of time to become defenders of the faith and repairers of the breach. The truth about the Creator and His lordship of the seventh-day Sabbath must go to the world in this generation.

We are living at the end of time. Damocles's sword dangles precariously above us. There is a world to warn. There is a generation to reach. There is a truth to tell. There is a faith to defend. There is a wall to repair—the protective wall of God's holy day and law. The final showdown will be over that breach in the wall of God's law. Mark these words. It will come down to that. For it will be an issue of authority— human tradition versus divine authority. Our mission is to repair the breach. For if that wall is not repaired, then the city will fall and all that are in it will be lost in the end.

"Repairers of the breach." *God needs a new generation of defenders of the faith.* And I earnestly appeal to you to answer His call and defend the faith of our Lord Jesus Christ to the very end.

> Once to every man and nation Comes the moment to decide,
> In the strife of truth with falsehood, For the good or evil side;
> Some great cause, God's new Messiah, Offering each the bloom or blight,

And the choice goes by forever 'Twixt that darkness and that light.

Then to side with truth is noble When we share her wretched crust,
Ere her cause bring fame and profit, And 'tis prosperous to be just;
Then it is the brave man chooses, While the coward stands aside,
Till the multitude make virtue Of the faith they had denied.

By the light of burning martyrs, Christ, Thy bleeding feet we track,
Toiling up new Calvaries ever With the cross that turns not back;
New occasions teach new duties, Time makes ancient good uncouth;
They must upward still and onward, Who would keep abreast of truth.

Though the cause of evil prosper, Yet 'tis truth alone is strong;
Though her portion be the scaffold, And upon the throne be wrong;
Yet that scaffold sways the future, And, behind the dim unknown,
Standeth God within the shadow, Keeping watch above His own.

—James Russell Lowell[2]

---

[1]Transcription of David Tasker's interview of Jim Manele, recorded July 2002. All quotations are from Pastor Manele during this interview.

[2]*Seventh-day Adventist Hymnal,* No. 606.

O Calcutta

T. S. Eliot once described how we may be "committing the greater treason by doing the right thing for the wrong reason." And what would be the *right* reason?

Ponder with me a solitary verse from Holy Scripture. Could *it* be the right reason? "The right reason for what?" you ask. "The right reason for the war in Iraq? The right reason for my career choice? The right reason for the woman I married? The right reason for the children we have? The right reason for church? The right reason for the research I'm doing? The right reason for the choices I make? Which *right* reason are you talking about?"

All of them, actually. Although I was really thinking of the right reason for Isaiah 58's impassioned appeal to serve the poor.. For you see, Eliot may be very right: We commit "the greater treason by doing the right thing for the wrong reason."

So, are you doing the right thing for the *right* reason? And what would be that *right* reason?

Here now is that solitary verse from the Bible: "You know how full of love and kindness our Lord Jesus Christ was. Though he was very rich, yet for your sakes he became poor, so that by his poverty he could make you rich" (2 Corinthians 8:9, NLT).

And where was it that this God went bankrupt for us, emptying His treasury to the last crimson penny? A second-century preacher, Melito of Sardis, described that place this way: "He who hung the earth in its place hangs there; he who fixed the heavens is fixed there; he who made all things fast is made fast upon the tree. The Master has been insulted; God has been murdered; the King of Israel has been slain by an Israelite hand. O strange murder, strange crime! The Master has been treated in unseemly fashion, his body naked, not even deemed worthy of a covering that his nakedness might not be seen. Therefore the lights of heaven turned away, and the day darkened, that it might hide him who was stripped upon the cross" (quoted in Richard John Neuhaus, *Death on a Friday Afternoon,* pp. 256, 257).

"For you know the grace of our Lord Jesus Christ, that though he was rich, yet for your sakes he became poor, so that you through his poverty might become rich" (2 Corinthians 8:9). The voluntary and ultimate impoverishment of Christ on the cross for us—how can our third-millennial minds possibly comprehend it! But at least we must try.

Imagine an amalgamation made of soggy cardboard and plastic bags propped up beside a filthy, putrid Calcutta gutter in the inner slums of that fetid city. You peer into its stinking, cramped, dingy interior, and you realize that it's someone's home! For there huddled in a fetal position is the wasted, bony form of a man, whose hollow eyes and sallow face stare back at you from above his protruding ribs and rotting flesh, the teeth left to him yellowed with decay as he pants to breathe.

You crawl into that hovel hellhole, and, holding your breath from the stench of diseased rot, you stoop over and scoop up the bony emaciated form of this semiconscious dreg of humanity. In your arms you bear him out of that dying slum to a waiting black and yellow taxi. You race to the Calcutta airport, carrying this gangrened stranger. You board a 747 and strap him into the seat beside you.

Twenty hours later and a half a world away, you land in Chicago— or New York or Los Angeles. And you drive back to your home. Still bearing that foul form of a man in your arms, you walk into your home— your room, your apartment, your mobile home, your duplex, your towering brick mansion. You *carry him in to where you live.* And there you bathe him, you cleanse him, you robe him, you feed him, you bed him down—this emaciated stranger—in your soft, clean linen bed for the night.

In the morning, when his bewildered eyes finally register the reality of the opulence that now surrounds him, you do a most unthinkable thing. In your hands are the keys to your room and house, your car, your SUV, your boat, your pantry. In your hands are the remote controls to your stereo, your VCR, your large-screen television. In your hand is also a file folder with the numbers to your checking and savings accounts, your credit cards, and your stock portfolios. You gaze into his face as you sweep your arms, pointing to your room and house. Then you heap your keys and remotes and accounts into the startled bosom of this rapidly recovering stranger. You shake his hand and hug his bony shoulders.

Then you take off your clothes and pick up his putrid, sticky loin cloth you removed the night before. And you wrap yourself in his decaying rags. Then with a final nod, you walk out of your room clutching only the return portion of the stranger's round trip ticket you had bought him. And boarding another 747, you fly a universe away—halfway around the world.

When you land back in Calcutta, you must walk now, you have no money; there'll be no taxi. Finally, hours and hours later, you come straggling into the very slum where you found him just days ago. By the retching smell you recognize the stranger's still rotten cardboard lean-to beside the putrid gutter. You have found his home. You then bend to the rancid ground and crawl on your bare hands and naked knees into that dank, dismal hole. And curling into a fetal position, you now live out the rest of your days on earth in that awful misery of abandoned filth.

And the stranger you rescued? He now possesses everything of yours—you gave it to him. And you now possess everything of his—he gave it to you. Your riches are now and forever his. And his poverty is now and forever yours.

" 'My God, my God—why have you forsaken me?' " (Matthew 27:46).

"You know how full of love and kindness our Lord Jesus Christ was. Though he was very rich, yet for your sakes he became poor, so that by his poverty he could make you rich" (2 Corinthians 8:9, NLT).

The Desire of Ages confirms it: "Christ was treated as we deserve, that we might be treated as He deserves. He was condemned for our sins, in which He had no share, that we might be justified by His righteousness, in which we had no share. He suffered the death which was ours, that we might receive the life which was His. 'With His stripes we are healed' " (p. 25).

Why should we, who were once poor and needy, love and serve the poor and needy? The reason could hardly be clearer: because the Jesus who became poor for us now calls us to become poorer for them. "Follow Me, for inasmuch as I have done it for you, you must do it for them."

Come to think of it, if we will follow Him, we shall never commit "the greater treason." For when we follow Jesus, we shall do the *right* thing for the *right* reason.

For didn't He somewhere once say, "Freely you have received, freely give"? (Matthew 10:8).

STUDY GUIDE
for
CHAPTER 1—THE LAW OF THE BOOKENDS

What do I think? *(Thought questions for individual reflection or group discussion)*

1. What do you think the author means by saying that God has chosen us, not because of who we are, but because of who He is? (See p. 16.) If that is true, what role do we have in accepting the assignment God has chosen for us?

2. Why does God place His call to mission in the context of doctrinal truths such as judgment and Sabbath? What relationship might there be between the "bookends"—judgment and the Sabbath—and God's call in Isaiah 58 to minister to others?

How do I feel? *(Check your attitude)*

1. When I read Isaiah 58:1 (God's "harsh introduction," as the author puts it), I:
   ❏ don't understand why the author feels that God's words are harsh in this verse.
   ❏ feel that I'm being unfairly accused by God if I apply this verse to myself.
   ❏ feel upset at how far my life falls short of what it should be.
   ❏ Other _____

2. When I read that God has chosen me to carry out His mission in the world, it makes me:

❏ want to learn His will for my life and perform it to the best of my ability by His grace.

❏ feel resentful that God is imposing a task on me that I haven't asked for.

❏ question whether God really expects every Christian to become involved in mission in a specific way.

❏ Other _____

What can I do? *(Practical plans for becoming involved)*

1. Is there a specific person in my family or neighborhood who I know is facing a particular problem right now? What resources do I have (am I willing to commit) to help solve that person's problem this week? If I don't have the resources myself, could I be a "broker" between someone who does and the person needing a solution?

What if . . . ? *(Dreaming, wishing, thinking outside the box)*

1. What would happen if I (my church) truly became passionate about helping those in need?

2. Is my church known in the community for its concern for those on the margins of society? If not, what would it take to change that perception?

What would Jesus do? *(Insights from the life of the Savior)*

1. Read Mark 6:35-44. What does this incident in Jesus' life tell us about the importance of ministering to people's physical needs compared to ministering to their spiritual needs? Can the two be separated? If so, should they be? If Jesus were on earth today, what kinds of issues would He be focusing on?

Further reading *(Sources for additional reflection)*

1. Ellen G. White, *Testimonies for the Church*, vol. 6, pp. 265–268.

STUDY GUIDE
for
CHAPTER 2—SMARTY-PANTS

What do I think? *(Thought questions for individual reflection or group discussion)*

1. Can we conclude from Matthew 25:31-46 that the question of how we have ministered to the needy is the *only* issue God will consider in the final judgment? What other issues, if any, does the Bible indicate will be involved in God's judgment on individuals?

2. What can (should) we conclude from the fact that Jesus had little in the way of material possessions when He lived on earth as a human? Is He an example for us in this regard? Is it not true that those who have material possessions are the ones who are best able to minister to the needy?

3. Must we choose between *knowing* the truth and *showing* the truth? Shouldn't the two be compatible? What might make it difficult for us or our church to carry out both?

How do I feel? *(Check your attitude)*

1. The author states, "Right behavior supercedes right belief" (p. 25).
   ❏ I agree. What a person does is always more important than what he or she believes.
   ❏ I disagree. What a person believes affects how they act. If a person is wrong in her or his beliefs, it's difficult for the actions to be correct.

❏ It depends. In some situations it's more important to act correctly than to have correct beliefs. In others, the reverse is true.
❏ Other _____

2. Belonging to a church that has the "truth" (has strong Bible evidence for its beliefs) is:
❏ important to me because one cannot sincerely follow Jesus and disregard Bible truth.
❏ less important to me than belonging to a church that follows Jesus' example of caring for the poor, the hungry, and the homeless.
❏ Other _____

What can I do? *(Practical plans for becoming involved)*
1. How can I emphasize Bible truth to neighbors and friends without coming across as a spiritual "know-it-all"?

What if . . . ? *(Dreaming, wishing, thinking outside the box)*
1. If I were a homeless person on the streets of a large city in America, what would I most like for a Christian or a church to do to help me? What would provide the most significant and long-term benefit? What actions would turn me off or cause me to misinterpret their motives?

What would Jesus do? *(Insights from the life of the Savior)*
1. Read John 8:32; 14:15, 23, 24. What do these texts imply about the way Jesus viewed the interaction between obedience (behavior) and correct doctrine (belief)?

Further reading *(Sources for additional reflection)*
1. Matthew 6:1-18; Ellen G. White, *Christ's Object Lessons*, pp. 150–163; *Thoughts From the Mount of Blessing*, pp. 79–88.

STUDY GUIDE
for
CHAPTER 3—THE CHAMPION

What do I think? *(Thought questions for individual reflection or group discussion)*

1. While on earth, Jesus seemed to indicate that the poor are more likely to be open to spiritual things than are the rich. Why should that be so? Cannot both wealth and grinding poverty cause a person to turn away from God? Does either riches or poverty, in itself, tend to draw a person toward spiritual things? Cannot both wealth and grinding poverty cause a person to turn away from God?

2. In what ways is Christ's earthly life, as described in the Gospels, an example that we should follow today? How far do we carry this? Does His example lie more in principles or in specifics?

3. Why, do you think, was Jesus such a champion of the poor when He was on earth? What group might He champion if He were on earth today?

How do I feel? *(Check your attitude)*

1. I believe that most of those who are living in poverty:
   ❏ could solve their financial problems by working harder and making better choices. Their situation is largely of their own making.
   ❏ are poor primarily because of forces in society beyond their control.
   ❏ deserve our concern and help regardless of the reasons for their poverty.

❏ Other _____

2. When I am confronted with an appeal for money:
  ❏ my first thought is whether the appeal is legitimate or a scam.
  ❏ I tend to give a small amount simply to avoid being bothered further.
  ❏ my inclination is to believe the person making the appeal and to help.
  ❏ Other _____

What can I do? *(Practical plans for becoming involved)*
1. Resolve to follow—for a week or a month—the author's suggestion in this chapter that Christians give something to *every* financial request that comes their way. Do this as a test of his assertion, "Nothing is so powerful an antidote to selfishness as unselfishness" (p. 48). Analyze the results on your life at the end of the test period.

What if . . . ? *(Dreaming, wishing, thinking outside the box)*
1. What if large numbers of Christians quit driving gas-guzzling SUVs? Or made lifestyle changes that sharply curtailed "conspicuous consumption" in other areas? Would all the effects be positive? In a highly industrialized economy built on consumer spending, could such moves cause unintended economic hardships and suffering that would be as harmful as the current situation? Are simple answers possible in the complicated economic world of today?

Further reading *(Sources for additional reflection)*
1. Luke 18:18-27. Did Jesus really mean what He said to the rich young ruler? Should we formulate universal principles from His words to specific individuals?

STUDY GUIDE
for
CHAPTER 4—TRAPPED IN THE SPIN CYCLE

What do I think? *(Thought questions for individual reflection or group discussion)*

1. What specific objections or problems would the church today encounter if it tried to follow the model of the early New Testament church in sharing all things in common? Do you think the early church encountered those same problems? Is this model viable over the long term? Why or why not?

2. What might be some implications of the idea that God's focus on helping the poor centers on the poor within our own community of faith?

3. This chapter suggests that a church in which members care for each others' physical/financial needs is a powerful force for attracting new members. Do you agree? Why or why not?

How do I feel? *(Check your attitude)*

1. If I knew someone in my church was in need (hungry, unable to pay the rent, etc.) I would:

❏ send him/her some money anonymously.

❏ get a number of friends to contribute money to help take care of the need.

❏ bring the need to the attention of the pastor.

❏ probably do nothing, especially if I felt the need was the result of poor judgment.

❏ Other _____

2. Jesus says that there will always be poor people in society and in the church. This means:
   ❏ the poor are an opportunity to exercise the golden rule.
   ❏ it is impossible to eradicate poverty no matter how hard we try.
   ❏ because poverty gives rise to numerous social problems, it is primarily an issue for the government to deal with—not the church.
   ❏ Other _____

What can I do? *(Practical plans for becoming involved)*
1. What responsibility do I have personally for individuals in my church who are in financial need? What if I am in need myself but still have more than some others?

What if . . . ? *(Dreaming, wishing, thinking outside the box)*
1. Would people be attracted to my Savior more by understanding His truth or by seeing His compassion demonstrated in the lives of His people? How could my church develop a model for evangelism built around ministry for the needy?

What would Jesus do? *(Insights from the life of the Savior)*
1. Read John 12:1-8. In these verses Jesus seems to approve spending a significant amount of money for purposes unrelated to helping the poor. What reasons can you think of why He might take such a position?

Further reading *(Sources for additional reflection)*
1. Acts 2:42-47; 5:1-11. Ellen G. White, *Acts of the Apostles,* pp. 70–76.

STUDY GUIDE
for
CHAPTER 5—THE SHABBAT SHALOM OF THE POOR

What do I think? *(Thought questions for individual reflection or group discussion)*

1. In helping the needy as God calls us to do in Isaiah 58, should we provide the needy with food, clothing, money, etc., or provide them with tools and skills to help themselves? Or both? Which requires more effort and long-term commitment? Which is most effective in dealing with poverty?

2. Why has the Seventh-day Adventist Church historically been reluctant to become seriously involved in "social justice" issues while at the same time it has emphasized helping individuals through community services programs?

3. What does God mean by saying that the "fast" He has chosen is to minister to the needy?

How do I feel? *(Check your attitude)*

1. Of the following statements, I agree most strongly with:
   ❏ It is never enough to have pity on the victims of injustice if we do nothing to change the unjust situation itself.
   ❏ Whatever you may possess above another places you in debt to all who are less favored.
   ❏ Without social justice, all the emphasis on doctrines won't fulfill God's mission on earth.

❏ To relieve the afflicted, to comfort the sorrowing, is a labor of love that does honor to God's holy day.

❏ Other _____

2. My ideal Sabbath would involve:

❏ worship, prayer, personal Bible study, meditation, and rest.

❏ worship, prayer bands, inviting others to Sabbath dinner, witnessing, ministering to others.

❏ Other _____

What can I do? *(Practical plans for becoming involved)*

1. The author gives a list of possible Sabbath afternoon activities in which you can present a gift from God to the needy (see pp. 65, 66). Which of these most appeals to you? What would you add to the list?

What if . . . ? *(Dreaming, wishing, thinking outside the box)*

1. What skills and expertise do the members of my church have that could be used to empower the poor and needy to break the cycle of poverty? How could I harness that expertise for action?

What would Jesus do? *(Insights from the life of the Savior)*

1. Read Matthew 12:9-14. How do Jesus' actions in this passage illustrate the statement the author puts in God's mouth, "You'll get My day right, only when you get My way right" (see p. 65)?

Further reading *(Sources for additional reflection)*

1. Ellen G. White, *Thoughts From the Mount of Blessing*, pp. 134–137.

STUDY GUIDE
for
CHAPTER 6—QUID PRO QUO

What do I think? *(Thought questions for individual reflection or group discussion)*

1. Are the promises God makes in Isaiah 58 (if you will do this, then I'll do that) supernatural blessings from Him or simply the "natural" results of certain actions and attitudes on our part?

2. What must be our motivation for ministering to the needy? Why does God emphasize the blessings that will be ours as a result of our ministering to others if that is not to be our motivation for service?

3. Are God's blessings conditional on our obedience? What insight do Matthew 5:45 and James 1:5-8 give on this question?

4. What is the source of the moral authority of figures such as Jimmy Carter, Mother Teresa, and Martin Luther King? Is this part of the blessings God promises to those who take seriously His concerns in Isaiah 58?

How do I feel? *(Check your attitude)*

1. Have you ever been manipulated or deceived by someone seeking help? How did that make you feel?
   ❏ Angry and unwilling to trust others who claim to be in need.
   ❏ Angry, but willing to be taken advantage of rather than to overlook someone in genuine need.

❏ Other _____

2. When I consider the promises God makes to those who minister to others, I:
   ❏ want to help others in order to experience the promised blessings.
   ❏ would help others even if God didn't offer blessings as a result.
   ❏ believe that the promised blessings are more spiritual than material.
   ❏ feel God offers us these blessings so that we can minister to others even more abundantly.
   ❏ Other _____

What can I do? *(Practical plans for becoming involved)*
1. Choose one activity listed in Isaiah 58 and think about how you could implement that specific action in practical ways in your everyday living.

What if . . . ? *(Dreaming, wishing, thinking outside the box)*
1. How might my life be different if I were to be more like the kind of Christian God is calling for in Isaiah 58? What changes would be required? What blessings might I expect?

What would Jesus do? *(Insights from the life of the Savior)*
1. Read John 3:16. What motivated Jesus to make this supreme sacrifice of self? Is there any benefit to Him?

Further reading *(Sources for additional reflection)*
1. Deuteronomy 28.

STUDY GUIDE
for
CHAPTER 7—THE TRUTH OF THE TALKING BULL

What do I think? *(Thought questions for individual reflection or group discussion)*

1. How does observance of the Sabbath help turn us away from the unchecked materialism that seems to characterize our modern society? What would be the result for society if individuals actually rested from their normal pursuits for a whole day each week?

2. Why do you think God links social justice issues with the Sabbath truth in Isaiah 58?

3. What is involved in repairing the "breach" in God's law—the truth of His Sabbath? Does it include more than calling the world to recognize the seventh day of the week as God's true Sabbath?

How do I feel? *(Check your attitude)*

1. For me, the most important blessing the Sabbath provides each week is:
   ❏ rest—physical and spiritual.
   ❏ worship time and fellowship with God's people.
   ❏ the opportunity to spend time ministering to others.
   ❏ permission to stop the mad rush of daily activity.
   ❏ Other _____

2. Do I truly feel that the Sabbath is a delight each week? Am I glad to see the sun setting on Friday evening?

3. When I think that God has called me to be a defender of the historic Christian faith:
   ❏ it makes me uneasy because I feel so inadequate to the task.
   ❏ I am not sure what the historic Christian faith is that I should be defending.
   ❏ I am willing to do what I can, trusting Jesus to lead me.
   ❏ Other _____

What can I do? *(Practical plans for becoming involved)*
1. What one thing about the Sabbath is most appealing to me? How can I enhance that aspect of the Sabbath and thus make the day more of a "delight" for me and my family?

2. How can I make Jesus the center of the Sabbath rest for me?

What if . . . ? *(Dreaming, wishing, thinking outside the box)*
1. What if God used miraculous means (such as a talking bull) more often in carrying out His mission on earth? Long term, would this have a positive or negative influence?

What would Jesus do? *(Insights from the life of the Savior)*
1. Read Luke 4:14-21. In what way was Isaiah 58 fulfilled in Jesus' life on earth?

Further reading *(Sources for additional reflection)*
1. 2 Kings 22; 23:1-30. What lessons for today can we learn from Josiah's efforts to direct God's people back to the "old paths"?

If you enjoyed this book, you'll enjoy this one

by Dwight Nelson:

The Eleventh Commandment

With memorable illustrations and a
powerful new parable for a
new millennium, author,
evangelist and pastor Dwight
Nelson shows us:

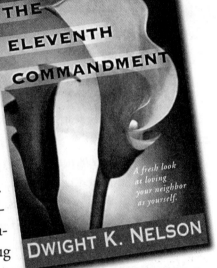

- The secrets of abiding in
  Christ and reflecting His
  love to a suffering world in
  desperate need.
- How the judgment revolves
  around showing love, not
  knowing the truth about love.
- How the eleventh commandment applies to an AIDS pa-
  tient, an unwed mother, a drug
  addict, and even a convicted sex
  offender.

Internalize these concepts and let this book launch you out of
your comfort zone into a radical new way of living and loving!
0-8163-1850-6. Paperback. US$4.97, Can$7.47.

Order from your ABC by calling **1-800-765-6955**, or get online
and shop our virtual store at **www.AdventistBookCenter.com**.

- Read a chapter from your favorite book
- Order online
- Sign up for email notices on new products